Android Quick APIs Reference

Onur Cinar

Apress®

Android Quick APIs Reference

Copyright © 2015 by Onur Cinar

ISBN-13 (pbk): 978-1-4842-0524-2

ISBN-13 (electronic): 978-1-4842-0523-5

Managing Director: Welmoed Spahr
Lead Editor: Steve Anglin
Technical Reviewer: Michael Thomas
Editorial Board: Steve Anglin, Louise Corrigan, James T. DeWolf, Jonathan Gennick,
    Robert Hutchinson, Michelle Lowman, James Markham, Matthew Moodie, Jeff Olson,
    Jeffrey Pepper, Douglas Pundick, Ben Renow-Clarke, Gwenan Spearing, Steve Weiss
Coordinating Editor: Melissa Maldonado
Copy Editor: Lori Jacobs
Compositor: SPi Global
Indexer: SPi Global
Artist: SPi Global
Cover Designer: Anna Ishchenko

Distributed to the book trade worldwide by Springer Science+Business Media New York, 233 Spring Street, 6th Floor, New York, NY 10013. Phone 1-800-SPRINGER, fax (201) 348-4505, e-mail orders-ny@springer-sbm.com, or visit www.springeronline.com. Apress Media, LLC is a California LLC and the sole member (owner) is Springer Science + Business Media Finance Inc (SSBM Finance Inc). SSBM Finance Inc is a Delaware corporation.

For information on translations, please e-mail rights@apress.com, or visit www.apress.com.

Apress and friends of ED books may be purchased in bulk for academic, corporate, or promotional use. eBook versions and licenses are also available for most titles. For more information, reference our Special Bulk Sales–eBook Licensing web page at www.apress.com/bulk-sales.

Any source code or other supplementary material referenced by the author in this text is available to readers at www.apress.com/9781484205242. For detailed information about how to locate your book's source code, go to www.apress.com/source-code/.

Dedicated to my son Deren, my wife Sema, and my parents, Zekiye and Dogan, for their love and their continued support.

—Onur Cinar

Contents at a Glance

Contents

About the Author

Onur Cinar is the author of *Android Apps with Eclipse* and *Pro Android C++ with the NDK*, and the co-author of *Android Best Practices*. He has over 19 years of experience in the design, development, and management of large-scale complex software projects, primarily in mobile and telecommunication space. His expertise spans VoIP, video communication, mobile applications, grid computing, and networking technologies on diverse platforms. He has been actively working with the Android platform since its beginning. He has a B.S. degree in Computer Science from Drexel University in Philadelphia, PA. He is currently working at the Skype division of Microsoft as the Principal Development Manager responsible for the Skype Qik, GroupMe, Skype for Android, and Lync for Android products.

About the Technical Reviewer

Michael Thomas has worked in software development for more than 20 years as an individual contributor, team lead, program manager, and Vice President of Engineering. Michael has over 10 years' experience working with mobile devices. His current focus is in the medical sector using mobile devices to accelerate information transfer between patients and health care providers.

Preface

Android is no longer just an operating system for mobile devices. It powers all sorts of connected devices, like TVs, and wearables. With its vast set of APIs (application programming interfaces), the Android platform enables endless opportunities for developers.

The Android Quick APIs Reference is a condensed code and API reference to the Android platform, including the new APIs that are introduced in Android Lollipop 5.0. It presents the essential Android APIs in a well-organized format that can be used as a handy reference.

The book extensively uses URLs to the official Android API Reference pages to enable you to dive into things as needed. The book is packed with useful information and is a must-have for any mobile or Android app developer or programmer.

What you'll learn

- Short introduction to the Android platform and its development environment.
- Essential parts of Android applications, such as the user interface components, the notifications, and the resources.
- Storing and accessing data using Android APIs.
- Accessing the location, and using device sensors.
- Recording and playing back video and audio content, and accessing the camera.

Who this book is for

This book is a quick, handy syntax reference for experienced Android programmers and a concise, easily digested introduction for other programmers new to Android.

Chapter 1

Android Platform

Android is a platform that is carefully crafted for mobile devices including smartphones, and tablets. It is a combination of an operating system, companion native libraries, application runtime, and an application framework. This chapter provides a brief introduction to the Android platform by emphasizing these key components and their roles in the overall system architecture. This book targets the 5.0 (Lollipop) version of the Android platform, which is the latest official version at the time of this writing.

Platform Architecture

Android relies on various open source technologies to provide a solid mobile platform that can satisfy mobile needs. The platform architecture can be best described as a series of five main layers that handle different core operations. Figure 1-1 shows the high-level architecture of the Android platform with these five main layers and their subcomponents.

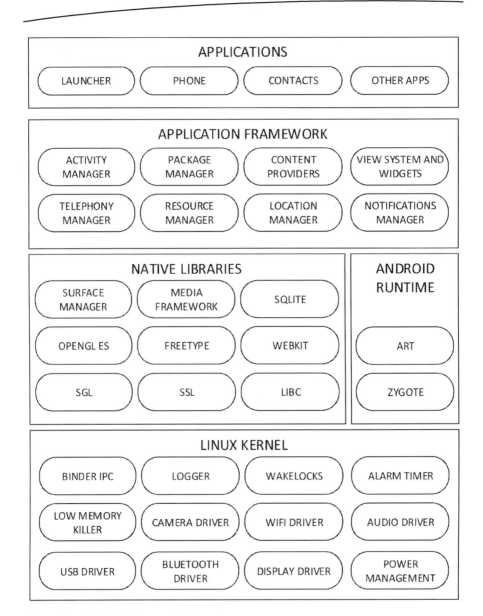

Figure 1-1. *Android platform architecture diagram*

This section will go through these five key layers starting from the bottom and moving upward.

Linux Kernel

The bottom layer of the Android platform is the Linux kernel. Android relies on the well-proven Linux kernel to provide its operating system functionality. Linux is a UNIX-like and Portable Operating System Interface (POSIX)-compliant operating system that is developed under a free open source software development model.

Android Inclusions

In order to satisfy the needs of mobile devices, Android's Linux kernel went through further architectural changes. This section briefly goes through the most notable inclusions in the Linux kernel.

Binder

The Android platform architecture makes heavy use of inter-process communication (IPC). Applications communicate with the system, phone, services, and each other by using IPC. As the IPC mechanism provided by the Linux operating system is not sufficient for mobile devices, the Android platform relies on its own IPC system, known as Binder. It is the central communication channel across the entire Android platform. As Binder is implemented as a low-level service in Android's Linux kernel, application developers are not expected to directly interact with it. The majority of the Android framework application programming interfaces (APIs) rely on Binder to interact with the platform in a way that is transparent to the application developer.

In order to use Binder to interact with other applications on the system, the Android Software Development Kit (SDK) provides the Android Interface Definition Language (AIDL).[1] AIDL allows the application developer to define the interface that both applications or the application and the service will use to communicate with each other. AIDL provides the functionality to decompose the passed objects into primitives that Binder can understand and use across process boundaries. You will learn more about AIDL in Chapter 3.

---

[1]http://developer.android.com/guide/components/aidl.html.

Logger

Logging is the most essential mechanism for troubleshooting. As mobile applications rely heavily on the environment surrounding them, such as the WiFi networks and the data coming from device sensors, application logs alone are simply not enough to troubleshoot complex problems. It is essential to combine logs coming from both the system and the application in order to draw a full picture.

This becomes even trickier to achieve on mobile platforms, where the development and the execution of the application happen on two different machines.

The Android platform provides a system-wide centralized logging service that can aggregate logs coming from the Android platform itself as well as the applications that are running on top of it.

The Android SDK also provides the necessary tools to monitor the logs in real-time with advanced filtering support.

Wake Locks

The Android platform is designed to operate on mobile devices with scarce resources. Battery power is the most important one. Because of this, Android devices frequently go into a low-powered mode, also known as sleep mode. Although this mode allows the system to use the available power reserve efficiently, it is not preferable for the device to go into sleep mode while a service or an application is in the middle of an important operation.

Wake locks were introduced into Android's Linux kernel in order to enable applications to prevent the device from going into sleep mode.

> **Caution**   Wake locks should be used carefully. Preventing the device from going into sleep mode will eventually cause it to run out of battery power. Applications should release the wake lock as soon as the important operation is complete.

Alarm Timer

As indicated in the "Wake Locks" section, Android devices go into sleep mode to conserve power. During sleep mode no Android applications can run; even the operating system is paused. In order to enable applications to schedule tasks for execution, the alarm timer was introduced into Android's Linux kernel. The alarm timer can wake up the device from sleep mode when a previously scheduled alarm goes off.

Low Memory Killer

Like power, memory is also a scarce resource on mobile devices. Besides the size of the memory, loading applications into memory is also a very costly operation. In order to overcome this issue, the Android platform keeps all started applications in memory even though the user is no longer interacting with them. This enables the user to quickly switch between applications.

This optimization comes with a cost: the device can quickly run out of memory as more and more applications get started. The low memory killer, also known as the Viking Killer, was introduced into Android's Linux kernel to manage and reclaim memory before the device runs out of memory.

As the available memory drops under a certain threshold, the low memory killer removes applications from memory starting with the least important one.

The importance of an application is defined by its visibility to the user. An application that is currently in the foreground is considered the most important application. Likewise, a backgrounded application is not considered important; its current state can be saved and later restored when the user navigates back to that application.

File System

The Android platform relies on Yet Another Flash File System (YAFFS2) as its primary file system format, as YAFFS2 is specifically designed to work on NAND-based flash chips.

The Android file system is also structured in a specific way to make it easier to upgrade different portions of the Android platform without impacting other parts. This is achieved by keeping different portions of the Android platform in different system partitions. This approach also makes the platform much more secure as the key components of the Android platform are not mutable during runtime, which prevents viruses and malware from infecting the key operating system components.

The partitions used depend on the device manufacturers. Following is a list of the most common partitions and their roles in the overall Android platform:

- /boot: Keeps the boot loader and the Linux kernel. This partition can only be modified during an upgrade, and it is not writable otherwise during runtime.

- /system: Keeps all Android system files and also the applications that are preloaded by the device manufacturer.

- /recovery: Keeps a recovery image to provide maintenance functionality in order to recover and restore the system.

- /data: Keeps the applications that are installed by the user, including the application data files. This partition is writable during runtime, but protected through file system permissions.

- /cache: Keeps frequently accessed and temporary files. On most Android devices this partition is kept only on random access memory (RAM) in order to serve the device quickly. Once the device reboots, the content of this partition gets lost as RAM is not persistent storage.

Native Libraries

On top of the Linux kernel layer, the Android platform contains a set of native libraries. The majority of the functionality that is exposed through the Android runtime layer is backed up by these native libraries. Most notable of them are

- SQLite: Provides an in-memory, relational SQL database to enable Android applications to easily persist and quickly access their data in a structured way.

- WebKit: Provides an HTML/CSS rendering and JavaScript execution engine, enabling Android applications to incorporate web technologies.

- OpenGL ES: Provides high-performance 2D and 3D rendering functionality.

- Open Core: Provides a media framework to enable Android applications to record and play back audio and video content.

- OpenSSL: Provides Secure Socket Layer (SSL) and Transport Level Security (TLS) protocols to enable Android applications to communicate securely with remote services through the use of cryptography.

Android Runtimes

The Android runtime is the portion that orchestrates the Android platform. The Android runtime runs the platform services as well as the applications that are running on top of the platform.

Android Runtime (ART)

The official programming language for Android is Java. Java is a general-purpose, object-oriented programming language that is specifically designed for platform-independent application development. Java achieves this by compiling the application code into an intermediate platform-independent interpreted language called bytecode. This bytecode gets executed through the Java Virtual Machine that is running on the platform.

The Android Runtime (ART) is the new Java Virtual Machine that was introduced experimentally in Android 4.4, and later with Android 5.0 became the official runtime for the Android applications. Prior to Android 5.0, Android applications used to run on the top of the Dalvik Virtual Machine (VM).

> **Note**   Although it is now being deprecated, applications that are targeting older versions of the Android platform should still test the application with the Dalvik VM to address any incompatibility problems.

Compared to the Dalvik VM's just-in-time (JIT) approach, ART relies on ahead-of-time (AOT) compilation to translate the bytecode into machine code during the installation of the application. This enables the application code to later be executed directly by the device's runtime environment.

Compiled Android Applications

Although ART is now the official runtime for the Android platform starting from Android 5.0, the majority of the Android devices that are running an older version of the Android platform rely on the Dalvik VM.

In order to produce application packages and binaries that are compatible with both ART and the Dalvik VM, Android application packages are still prepared based on Dalvik specifications. As it was optimized for mobile, the Dalvik VM understands only a special type of bytecode which is known as Dalvik Executable (DEX). The Android SDK comes with tools that can translate standard Java bytecode into DEX bytecode during the packaging of the Android application. DEX bytecode provides lots of advantages compared to standard Java bytecode. ART does an automatic conversion from Dalvik's DEX format into ART's OAT format on the fly as soon as an application is installed on the device.

Application Sandbox

The Android platform is built with security in mind as an important requirement. It runs every application in a sandbox by isolating application data and code execution from other applications.

- Each application runs on its own dedicated ART VM instance.

- Application data is protected through the use of file system permissions. Each application gets assigned an account at installation, and the operating system restricts access to the application data for that account.

- Applications can only communicate with the system and with other applications through the communication interfaces that the Android platform provides. These interfaces are also protected through Android permissions.

Zygote

Zygote, also known as the "app process," is the parent of all Android application processes. It is one of those core processes started when the system boots. Zygote has two important roles.

- Once the system boots, Zygote starts a new ART VM instance and initializes the core Android services: Power, Telephony, Content, and Package.

▓ As noted, on the Android platform, every application runs within a dedicated ART VM instance. It is a very costly operation to start a new ART VM instance and load the Android framework components into memory for every Android application. Zygote solves this problem through the use of forking. When a user requests a new application, Zygote simply forks itself. Upon forking, the existing Zygote process gets cloned as a new process. Both the Zygote process and the new process share the pre-loaded Android framework resources. This allows applications to start very quickly, and also with a much smaller footprint.

> **Note**   In computing, forking is the operation to clone an existing process. The new process has an exact copy of the forked process, although both processes execute independently. Forking allows both processes to share the same memory segment until one of them tries to modify it.

Application Framework

The Application framework runs on the top of the ART VM and provides an interface to Android applications to interact with the Android platform and the device. It provides services such as Package Manager, Telephony Manager, Location Manager, and Notifications Manager.

Applications

The application space contains all user-facing Android applications that are running on top of the ART VM. Those applications include both third-party applications that are downloaded from Android markets and system applications such as Launcher, Contacts, Phone, and Browser. This book will show you how to use the Android framework APIs to develop Android applications that will execute within the **application space**.

Android Versions

When speaking of Android, you will often hear the same Android version being referred to in many different ways.

- This application requires *Jelly Bean* and above.

- My phone finally got the *Android 4.1* update.

- The Network Service Discovery Manager is available starting from Android *API Level 16*.

This section discusses each of these different version schemes and how they relate to each other. Table 1-1 provides a reference to easily map between those version schemes.

Platform Version

The Android platform is versioned using the change significance version scheme. The platform version number consists of two- or three-integer sequence identifiers that are separated by dots, such as Android *4.0.3*.

The first identifier in the platform version number denotes the major version number and is incremented only for releases with significant functionality changes. The second and third identifiers are for minor version numbers and they are incremented for minor changes and bug fixes. Based on that, an update from Android 3.2 to Android 4.0 indicates a major release, and an update from Android 4.0 to Android 4.0.1 represents a minor bug fix release.

At the time of this writing, the latest Android platform version is 5.0. The Android platform has gone through a number of updates and bug fixes since the first commercial use of Android 1.0 on September 23, 2008.

Platform Codename

As the target audience for the Android platform is not only developers, since April 2009, each major Android platform version has been released under a codename based on desserts such as KitKat, Jelly Bean, Ice Cream, and Lollipop.

API Level

Although the minor bug fix releases are usually transparent from the application developer's perspective, the major platform updates usually mean changes and additions to the Android framework API.

In order to make this concept easier to follow, the Android framework API is versioned separately from the Android platform through an integer identifier known as the API level. Each Android platform version supports exactly one API level, and the lower API levels are supported implicitly.

On the Android Developers Portal, API documentation always provide the API level where the API was introduced, as shown in Table 1-1 in order to make the developer aware of the API level requirement.

Table 1-1. Android Release Dates, Platform Versions, Codenames, and API Levels

Release Date	Platform Version	Platform Codename	API Level
September 2008	1.0	--	1
February 2009	1.1	--	2
April 2009	1.5	Cupcake	3
September 2009	1.6	Donut	4
October 2009	2.0	Éclair	5
December 2009	2.0.1	Éclair	6
January 2010	2.1	Éclair	7
May 2010	2.2–2.2.3	Froyo	8
December 2010	2.3–2.3.2	Gingerbread	9
February 2011	2.3.3–2.3.7	Gingerbread	10
February 2011	3.0	Honeycomb	11
May 2011	3.1	Honeycomb	12
July 2011	3.2–3.2.6	Honeycomb	13
October 2011	4.0–4.0.2	Ice Cream Sandwich	14
December 2011	4.0.3–4.0.4	Ice Cream Sandwich	15
July 2012	4.1–4.1.2	Jelly Bean	16
November 2012	4.2–4.2.2	Jelly Bean	17
July 2013	4.3–4.3.1	Jelly Bean	18
October 2013	4.4–4.4.4	KitKat	19
July 2014	4.4w	KitKat with Wearable Extensions	20
November 2014	5.0	Lollipop	21

You can use Table 1-1 as a reference to map between these three different version schemes.

The Android platform is very actively being developed. As shown in Table 1-1, over the course of four years, the Android platform went through a large number of update and bug fix releases.

Android Platform Fragmentation

By simply glancing through the release dates shown in Table 1-1, you might think that most of the Android devices out there must be running at least Android 4.4, as it has been out for a year; however, this is not true. Due to high fragmentation, the release dates do not provide a clear view of the Android ecosystem.

Table 1-2 is the latest version distribution chart from *Android Platform Versions Dashboard*[2] based on the data collected in December 2014.

Table 1-2. Android platform version distribution chart

Platform Version	Platform Codename	API Level	Distribution
2.2–2.2.3	Froyo	8	0.5%
2.3.3–2.3.7	Gingerbread	9	9.1%
4.0.3–4.0.4	Ice Cream Sandwich	15	7.8%
4.1–4.1.2	Jelly Bean	16	21.3%
4.2–4.2.2	Jelly Bean	17	20.4%
4.3–4.3.1	Jelly Bean	18	7.0%
4.4–4.4.4	KitKat	19	33.9%

At the time of this writing, the latest version of the Android platform to be out for any length of time, Android 4.4, is only 33.9% of the overall Android user base. Developing an Android application targeting only API Level 19 will limit the application's audience only to that 33.9% portion of the entire Android user base.

There are 21 API levels that you should consider while developing your application; make sure to take the version distribution chart in to consideration. Although higher API levels provide additional functionality, they also determine the size of your audience.

---

[2]https://developer.android.com/about/dashboards/index.html.

Android Support Library

Although targeting a lower API level increases the audience of your application, it also limits the Android platform features that you can use within your application. In order to overcome this trade-off, the Android Support Library has been introduced. The Android Support Library package is a set of code libraries that provide backward-compatible versions of recent Android APIs. This means that your application can benefit from an Android API that is only available in API Level 19 but can still target devices running API Level 4 and up. Including the Android Support Library in your Android application is considered a best practice for Android application development.

> **Note**   The Android Support Library does not cover every new API, as some of them may require additional operating system features that are only supported by a specific Android platform release.

Each Android Support Library targets a different base API level and based on that provides a different set of backward-compatible API features. You should choose the support library flavor based on the set of features that you will need. The *Support Library Feature Guide*[3] provides an overview of support library flavors from which you can choose.

In the next chapters, you will learn how to include the Android Support Library in your Android application.

Summary

This first chapter of the book covered the fundamentals of the Android platform. As indicated earlier in this chapter, you will not be directly interfacing with most of the core components that are presented in the section "Platform Architecture," although knowing these components will make it easier for you to understand the Android framework functions that will be covered in the next few chapters.

---

[3]http://developer.android.com/tools/support-library/features.html.

Chapter **2**

Development Environment

Android has a complete and advanced development environment that can run on all major operating systems.

Android Toolchain

The Android Open Source Project (AOSP) provides a comprehensive development toolchain for application developers.

The AOSP builds the entire development environment by integrating carefully chosen existing open source development tools, thereby creating this comprehensive toolchain. This approach enables application developers to develop mobile applications using the tools with which they are already familiar.

The Android toolchain is formed by four main components. This section discusses each of the key components.

Android Software Development Kit

The Android Software Development Kit (SDK) is the key component of the Android toolchain. The Android SDK provides

- Platform API Java Libraries
- An Application Packager
- Device Emulators
- A Bytecode Optimizer and Obfuscator

- An Android Debug Bridge
- Sample Code and Tutorials
- Platform Documentation

The Android SDK is the only required component for developing Android applications.

Android Native Development Kit

As indicated in Chapter 1, the Android platform relies on the Linux kernel to provide its operating system functionality. The combination of the Linux kernel and the BSD C library provides all the necessary pieces to execute platform-dependent, non-Java application code.

This makes it possible to develop performance-critical portions of Android applications using machine code generating programming languages such as C, C++, and assembly. Besides its performance advantages, this approach is frequently used for bringing existing legacy or shared code to the Android platform without rewriting it in Java.

The Android Native Development Kit (NDK) provides a companion tool set for the Android SDK, designed to enable developers to build and embed native code seamlessly within Java-based applications.

The Android NDK consists of cross compilers, debuggers, platform header files, and extensive documentation.

Android Development Tools for Eclipse

The Android Development Tools (ADT) for Eclipse were the first attempt to provide an integrated development environment (IDE) that is tailored for Android application development. As with the other components of the Android toolchain, this was achieved by providing customizations and additional features on the top of the Eclipse IDE platform.

Android Studio

On May 16, 2013, Google announced *ANDROID STUDIO*[1], a new IDE for Android development. Android Studio is also a customized IDE experience based on *INTELLIJ IDEA*. Android Studio provides some additional features

---

[1]http://developer.android.com/sdk/installing/studio.html.

and improvements over *Eclipse ADT* such as support for build variants and a rich user interface (UI) layout editor. The first stable version of Android Studio, version 1.0, was released in December 2014.

As Android Studio is the official Android IDE moving forward, this book uses Android Studio instead of Eclipse ADT.

Setting Up the Development Environment

In this section, you will learn how to successfully install Android Studio on your machine. Android Studio is available for all major operating systems (OSs), including Windows, Mac OS X, and Linux. Android Studio comes prepackaged with the Android SDK, making the environment setup simpler and easier for developers.

The only prerequisites for Android Studio are the *Java Development Kit (JDK)* and the *Java Runtime Edition (JRE)*. The Android development toolchain supports multiple JDK and JRE flavors, such as Open JDK, IBM JDK, and Oracle JDK (formerly known as Sun JDK). In order to keep the chapters of this book platform agnostic, it is assumed that the Oracle JDK will be used.

Although both Java versions 6 and 7 are supported by the Android toolchain, I recommend that you install Java 7 in order to be ready for upcoming Android platforms.

> **Caution**   As the Android platform evolves very rapidly, the requirements and the versions of the Android development toolchain components may have changed since this book was published. You should check the Android Studio home page for the latest information and requirements.

As the requirements and installation instructions vary, this section covers each OS separately.

Microsoft Windows

On Microsoft Windows, both Android Studio and the Java platform come with installation packages. The installation wizards will guide you through the process of installing both applications easily.

Downloading and Installing JDK on Windows

1. Using your web browser, navigate to Oracle's
    Java download web page at `www.oracle.com/`
    `technetwork/java/javase/downloads/index.html`.
    This page presents you with a list of download
    options.

2. Scroll down to the Java 7 section.

3. Click the JDK button to download the Java 7 installer
    application. At the time of this writing, the latest
    version of Java 7 is Update 71.

4. The Java 7 installation wizard will install both the
    JDK and the JRE. Throughout this process, you can
    proceed with the default values.

The installation wizard will automatically perform the necessary system
changes to make both the JDK and JRE available to Windows applications,
including Android Studio.

Downloading and Installing Android Studio on Windows

1. Using your web browser, navigate to the Android
    Studio download page at `http://developer.`
    `android.com/sdk/installing/studio.html`.

2. The web site will detect your OS, and it will show you
    the Android Studio download button for your OS.

3. Click the download button to download the Android
    Studio installer. At the time of this writing, the latest
    version of Android Studio is 1.0.1.

4. The Android Studio installation wizard will guide
    you through the process. You can continue with the
    default values throughout the installation process.

Android Studio is now ready to use. In the next section, you will be building
a small Android application to validate your installation.

Apple Mac OS X

On Mac OS X, both Android Studio and the Java platform come with installer applications.

Downloading and Installing JDK on Mac OS X

1. Using your web browser, navigate to Oracle's Java download web page at www.oracle.com/ technetwork/java/javase/downloads/index.html. This page presents you with a list of download options.

2. Scroll down to the Java 7 section.

3. Click the JDK button to download the Java 7 disk image. At the time of this writing, the latest version of Java 7 is Update 71.

4. Once the download is complete, double click the Java 7 disk image to mount it. The disk image contains the Java 7 installation application.

5. The Java 7 installation wizard will install both the JDK and the JRE. Throughout this process, you can proceed with the default values.

The installation wizard will automatically perform the necessary system changes to make both the JDK and JRE available to Windows applications, including Android Studio.

Downloading and Installing Android Studio on Mac OS X

1. Using your web browser, navigate to the Android Studio download page at http://developer. android.com/sdk/installing/studio.html.

2. The web site will detect your OS, and it will show you the Android Studio download button for your OS.

3. Click the download button to download the Android Studio disk image. At the time of this writing, the latest version of Android Studio is 1.0.1.

4. Once the download is complete, double click the Android Studio disk image.

5. Drag and drop the Android Studio icon onto the Applications icon to install Android Studio.

Android Studio is now ready to use. In the next section, you will be building a small Android application to validate your installation.

Ubuntu Linux

Compared to Microsoft Windows and Mac OS X, neither Android Studio nor the Java platform comes with an installation application. Both applications are available for Linux as compressed TAR archive files. This section goes through the steps that are necessary to successfully install Android Studio on Linux.

1. In order to make it easier to set up the environment, this section assumes that all Android toolchain components, including the Java 7 platform, will be installed in a new subdirectory, android, under the user's home directory. Open a Terminal window, and issue `mkdir ~/android` to create the new subdirectory.

2. Change the current directory to the new android directory by issuing cd `~/android` on the command prompt.

Downloading and Installing JDK on Linux

1. Using your web browser, navigate to Oracle's Java download web page at `www.oracle.com/technetwork/java/javase/downloads/index.html`. This page presents you with a list of download options.

2. Scroll down to the Java 7 section.

3. Click the JDK button to download the Java 7 compressed TAR archive file. At the time of this writing, the latest version of Java 7 is Update 71.

4. Once the download is completed, extract the Java 7 platform archive file under the ~/android subdirectory by issuing tar zxf ~/Downloads/jdk-7u71-linux-i586.tar.gz. Substitute the file name based on the name of the Java 7 archive file that you have downloaded.

Downloading and Installing Android Studio on Linux

1. Using your web browser, navigate to the Android Studio download page at http://developer. android.com/sdk/installing/studio.html.

2. The web site will detect your OS, and it will show you the Android Studio download button for your OS.

3. Click the download button to download the Android Studio compressed TAR archive. At the time of this writing, the latest version of Android Studio is 1.01.

4. Once the download is completed, extract the Android Studio archive file under the ~/android subdirectory by issuing tar xvf ~/Downloads/android-studio-bundle-135.1641136-linux.tgz.

5. You can now start Android Studio by issuing ~/android/android-studio/studio.sh on the command prompt.

Hello Android Application

Android Studio is now ready. In this section you will be building a Hello Android application to verify the Android toolchain installation.

Creating a New Android Application Project

To create a new project, complete the following steps:

1. When you start Android Studio for the first time, Quick Start dialog will be displayed as shown in Figure 2-1.

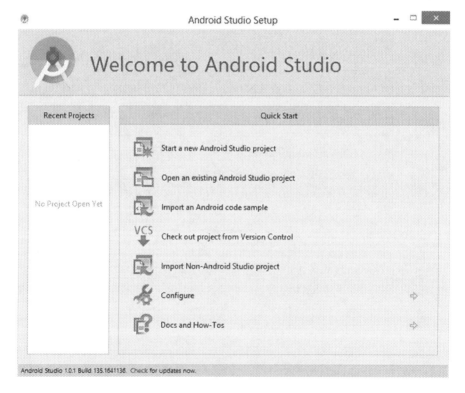

Figure 2-1. Android Studio Quick Start

2. Click the New Project menu item to proceed.

3. The new Android application project dialog will be displayed as shown in Figure 2-2.

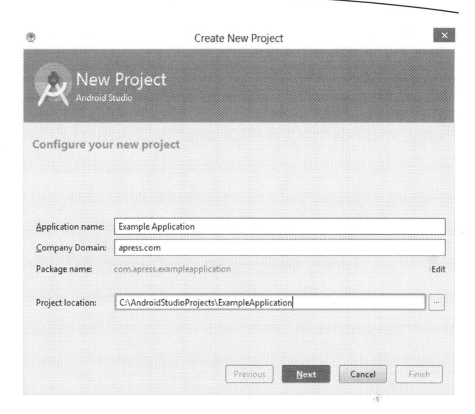

Figure 2-2. New Android application dialog

4. Set *APPLICATION NAME* to **Hello Android**.

5. Set *COMPANY DOMAIN* to **apress.com**.

6. Click the Next button to proceed.

7. As shown in Figure 2-3, on the next screen Android Studio will ask you to choose the target application programming interface (API) level for the new Android application project. Choose API Level 21 for Android 5.0 Lollipop.

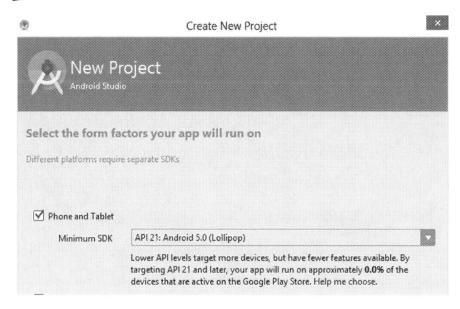

Figure 2-3. *Target Android API level*

8.   As shown in Figure 2-4, select Blank Activity on the next screen, and click the Next button to proceed.

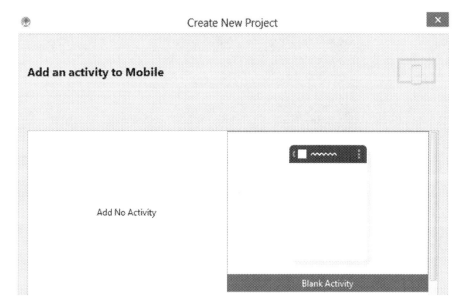

Figure 2-4. *Android project activity type*

9. As shown in Figure 2-5, continue with the default
    values for the new activity.

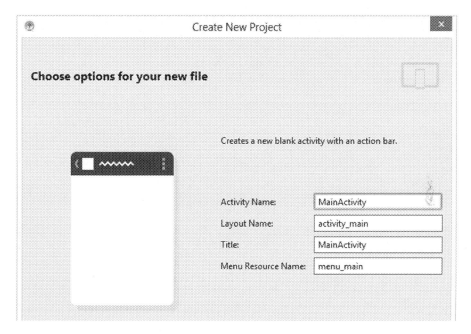

Figure 2-5. Activity name

10. Click the Finish button to complete the New Android
    Project Wizard.

11. Android Studio will open the new project in edit
    mode as shown in Figure 2-6.

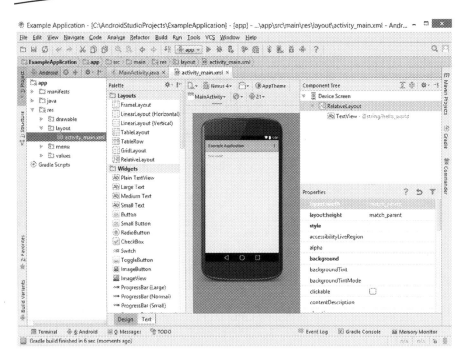

Figure 2-6. The new Android project editor

Building the Android Application

The new Android application project can be built by choosing Build ➤ Make Project from the top menu bar of the Android Studio.

Running the Android Application

Once the Android application project is built, it can run on both the actual Android devices and the Android emulator that comes as part of the Android toolchain.

The Android application can run on any Android device, as long as the attached Android device runs a version of the Android platform that is greater than or equal to the minimum target API level that is specified for the application.

Enabling USB Debug Mode on the Android Device

For Android Studio to see and communicate with the attached Android device, the USB Debug mode should first be enabled on the device itself. Different versions of the Android platform allow the developers to do this in different ways.

Using your Android device, running Android 4.2 or greater, take the following steps to enable the USB Debug mode:

1. Before you start, make sure that the Android device is not yet connected to the developer machine through the USB cable.

2. Using the Android device, go to the *SETTINGS* screen.

3. Scroll down to the *ABOUT* menu item.

> **Note**   On Samsung Galaxy devices, first choose *MORE/GENERAL*, then choose *ABOUT*.

4. On the *ABOUT* screen, scroll down to *BUILD NUMBER*.

5. Tap on *BUILD NUMBER* exactly seven times.

6. If the previous step is successful, you will see a toast message saying "*DEVELOPER MODE HAS BEEN ENABLED*."

7. Now go back to the Settings screen.

8. Scroll down and you should now see a new menu item, *DEVELOPER OPTIONS*. Choose that menu item.

9. On the *DEVELOPER OPTIONS* screen, check *USB DEBUGGING*.

10. Now plug the Android device into the developer machine through the USB cable.

11. Once the Android device connects to the developer machine, the device will show dialog asking your permission to allow the USB debug connection.

12. Accept that request to proceed.

Now the Android device is configured to allow Android Studio to execute Android applications.

> **Note**   As these steps may be different on your Android device, please check www.droidviews.com/how-to-enable-developer-optionsusb-debugging-mode-on-devices-with-android-4-2-jelly-bean/ for more recipes on how to enable the USB Debug mode on some other Android devices.

Running the Application on the Android Device

From the top menu bar, choose Run ➤ Run 'app' to launch the Choose Device dialog.

As shown in Figure 2-7, the Choose Device dialog will be launched to display the list of attached Android devices on which you can run the Android application.

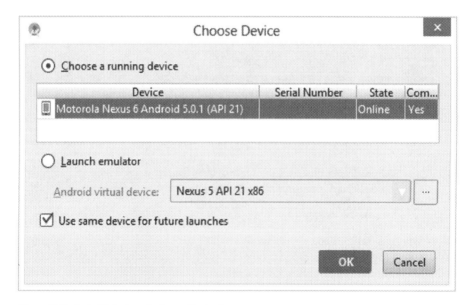

Figure 2-7. Android devices that are attached

Select the Android device you want to use and click the OK button to start the application on the selected Android device.

For the Android device to show up on this list, the USB Debug mode should be enabled on that device through the Developer Options settings page.

> **Note**   In addition to the actual Android devices, Android Studio also
> can run Android applications on an Android emulator that is running on
> the same development machine. To run the application on the Android
> emulator, simply select the Launch Emulator option in the Choose Device
> dialog and then choose an Android virtual device from the dropdown
> menu. Other Android emulator flavors also can be created using the AVD
> Manager button on the toolbar.

Summary

The Android platform provides a comprehensive development toolchain for
application developers. In this chapter, you have learned how to successfully
set up the Android development environment, including creating, building,
and running an Android application on both the attached Android device
and the Android emulator instance. The next chapter will go through the
anatomy of an Android application.

Chapter 3

Application Components

The Android framework provides a set of components to enable the development of consistent and interoperable mobile applications. In this chapter you will learn about these fundamental components and what they provide.

Activity

"Activity" is the name given to a single application window with which the user can interact at any given time. As Android applications run full screen on a limited display space, the name "activity" is given to an application window to reflect that it can only deliver a single and focused experience to the end user.

On the Android platform, this approach of limiting the scope of every screen also makes it possible for applications to deliver a functionality by blending activities from other applications. Imagine your e-mail client on your Android device seamlessly blending the contact list activity into the flow for sending an e-mail. This makes it possible to code less and maintain unity of the entire platform by promoting reuse. You will learn more about communicating between applications in the section "Intents."

Almost all activities require interaction with the user, and for that reason, the activity takes care of creating the window and laying out the user interface (UI) components. You will learn more about the various UI components available for your application in Chapter 4.

Creating an Activity

You can create a new activity simply by deriving a new class from the android.app.Activity[1] class as shown in Listing 3-1.

Listing 3-1. Creating a New Android Activity

```
package com.apress.helloworld;

import android.app.Activity;

public class MyActivity extends Activity {

}
```

Declaring an Activity

Deriving an Activity class does not make the new activity available automatically. As activities can take different roles in an application, the Android platform requires some meta information about the new activity. This meta information needs to be provided as part of the Android manifest file through the <activity>[2] XML tag, as shown in Listing 3-2.

Listing 3-2. Declaring the New Activity in the AndroidManifest.xml File

```
<?xml version="1.0" encoding="utf-8"?>
<manifest xmlns:android="http://schemas.android.com/apk/res/android"
    package="com.apress.helloworld" >

    <application
        android:allowBackup="true"
        android:icon="@drawable/ic_launcher"
        android:label="@string/app_name"
        android:theme="@style/AppTheme" >
<activity
android:name=".MyActivity"
android:label="@string/app_name" >
<intent-filter>
<action android:name=
"android.intent.action.MAIN" />
<category android:name=
```

---

[1]http://developer.android.com/reference/android/app/Activity.html.
[2]http://developer.android.com/guide/topics/manifest/activity-element.html.

```
"android.intent.category.LAUNCHER" />
</intent-filter>
</activity>
    </application>
</manifest>
```

As shown in Listing 3-2, the `<activity>` XML tag declares the new activity by providing its class name, its title, and how it should be exposed to the user.

Activity Life Cycle

The life cycle of an activity is the group of states that an activity goes through from the time it is first created until it is destroyed.

> **Caution**   The life cycle of the Android platform is much more complicated than the life cycle of ordinary desktop applications. The life cycle of desktop applications is directly under the user's control. On Android, the platform manages the life cycle of Android components in order to effectively use scarce system resources.

An activity goes through seven life cycle states. The activity becomes informed about life cycle state changes through a set of life cycle hooks defined in the `Activity` class. Application developers can override those hooks to do appropriate work when the activity changes its state. Listing 3-3 shows these methods.

Listing 3-3. Activity Life Cycle Hooks That Can Be Overridden

```
public class MyActivity extends Activity {
    protected void onCreate(Bundle savedInstanceState);
    protected void onStart();
    protected void onRestart();
    protected void onResume();
    protected void onPause();
    protected void onStop();
    protected void onDestroy();
}
```

Figure 3-1 illustrates the order in which these hooks will get called by the Android platform as the activity goes through life cycle states.

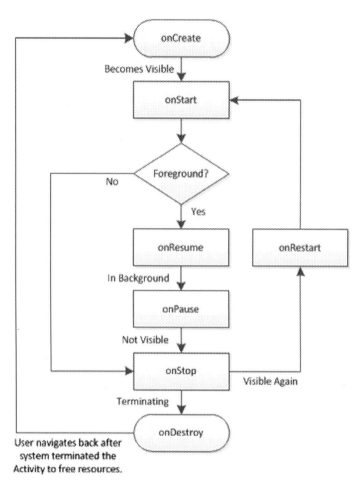

Figure 3-1. Activity life cycle state machines

Caution   When overriding these life cycle hooks, make sure to invoke the super class's implementation first. Not doing that may cause random faulty behavior during application runtime.

▨ onCreate is called when the activity gets created. All activities implement this method in order to initialize the activity and its UI. This method also takes an android. os.Bundle[3] object that may contain the frozen state from the previous run of this activity. At this stage the activity is not yet visible to the user.

Note   A bundle is used to carry data between activities, services, and even applications on Android. It is an Android construct that holds plain data as a map of key/value pairs. The stored data is serialized into a byte stream by the platform and later is deserialized into proper objects when restored. This type of data is known as a Parcel[4] on the Android platform.

▨ onStart is called when the activity becomes visible to the user. Although the activity is now visible, the user still cannot interact with it until the application is foregrounded.

▨ onResume is called when the activity is foregrounded. At this state, the user can interact with the application.

▨ onPause is called when the activity is no longer in the foreground. As the user may not come back, the activity is expected to save its current state into a bundle.

▨ onStop is called when the activity is no longer visible to the user.

▨ onRestart is called if the activity becomes visible again. The onStart method gets called next.

▨ onDestroy is called when the platform is destroying the activity.

Caution   After the onStop or onDestroy methods return, the platform may decide to kill the application process at any time. Activities are expected to save their current state during the call to the onPause method.

---

[3]http://developer.android.com/reference/android/os/Bundle.html.
[4]http://developer.android.com/reference/android/os/Parcel.html.

Intent

As mentioned earlier in the Activity section, the Android platform is designed to be highly modular, promoting collaboration among the applications that are present on the device. Applications can blend activities from each other to provide a certain functionality to the user. This is achieved through a late runtime binding facility, known as `android.content.Intent`,[5] which the Android framework provides.

The intent holds a passive data structure that holds an abstract description of an action to be performed. The primary pieces of information in an intent are

- `action`, which is the general action to be performed, such as `ACTION_VIEW`, `ACTION_EDIT`.

- `data`, which is a URI (uniform resource identifier) object that refers to the data to be acted on, such as `content://contacts/people/1`, `tel:6501231234`.

The optional information pieces in an intent are

- `type`, which is the MIME type for the data.

- `component`, which explicitly names the component, such as a specific activity, that should handle the action.

- `extras`, which are a bundle that carries additional information for the action as a key/value pair.

The most significant use of an intent is to launch activities and services. Listing 3-4 demonstrates how you can launch the contact list activity to enable the user to browse through the contacts.

Listing 3-4. Code to Launch the Contact List Through an Intent

```
Intent intent = new Intent();
intent.setAction(Intent.ACTION_VIEW);
intent.setData(Uri.parse("content://contacts/people/"));

startActivity(intent);
```

---

[5]`http://developer.android.com/reference/android/content/Intent.html`.

Intent Resolution

Once the intent is created and dispatched through the Android framework, the Android platform resolves the intent to find candidates that can provide the requested action. There are two main groups of intents that define how they get resolved and dispatched.

- **Explicit intents** are intents with an explicitly specified component, as shown in Listing 3-5. These intents automatically get dispatched to the specified component.

Listing 3-5. Intent with an Explicitly Specified Component

```
Intent intent = new Intent();
intent.setAction(Intent.ACTION_VIEW);
intent.setComponent(new ComponentName(
                    "com.apress",
                    "com.apress.MyActivity"));

startActivity(intent);
```

- **Implicit intents** are intents that do not specify a component. Based on the information provided in the intent, the Android platform goes through all of the installed application's intent filters to come up with the best matches that can fulfill the requested action.

Intent Filters

Intent filters allow the application to declare the list of intents that it can fulfill. It is declared in the application's manifest file, `AndroidManifest.xml`. Going back to Listing 3-2, you will recall that MyActivity declared the following intent filter:

```
<activity
    android:name=".MyActivity"
    android:label="@string/app_name" >
    <intent-filter>
        <action android:name=
                "android.intent.action.MAIN" />
        <category android:name=
                "android.intent.category.LAUNCHER" />
    </intent-filter>
</activity>
```

This intent filter instructs the Android platform that this activity should be included in the resolution of Launcher activities. This way, the icon of the new application gets shown on the Launcher screen for the user to be able to start it.

Multiple intent filters can be declared for a single activity as well. For example, if this activity can fulfill a request to play a video file, it can declare an intent filter similar to the following:

```
<activity
    android:name=".MyActivity"
    android:label="@string/app_name" >
 <intent-filter>
 <action android:name=
 "android.intent.action.MAIN" />
 <category android:name=
 "android.intent.category.LAUNCHER" />
 </intent-filter>

 <intent-filter>
 <action android:name=
 "android.intent.action.VIEW" />
 <category android:name=
 "android.intent.category.DEFAULT" />
 <data android:mimeType="video/*" />
 </intent-filter>
</activity>
```

As indicated earlier, intents are not only used to launch activities. In this chapter you will learn how to use intents to interact with services and broadcast messages. Intent filters can also be created through code using the android.content.IntentFilter[6] class; you will see an example in the section "Broadcast Messages."

Getting and Extracting the Intent

Once the intent is properly dispatched and the activity gets started, the newly started activity gets hold of the intent by using the getIntent() method of the Activity class, as shown in Listing 3-6.

---

[6]http://developer.android.com/reference/android/content/IntentFilter.html.

Listing 3-6. Accessing the Intent That Started the Activity

```
Intent intent = getIntent();

Uri data = intent.getData();

if (intent.getAction().equals(Intent.ACTION_VIEW)) {
    // view action
} else if (intent.getAction().equals(Intent.ACTION_EDIT)) {
    // edit action
}
```

Pending Intent

Although intents are mostly used to start an operation, they are also used for registering callbacks.

> **Note** A "callback" in computer programming refers to a reference to a function that is passed as an argument to another code, which is expected to call back the originating code by executing the referenced code at some time in the future. It is mostly used to sign up to be notified for events.

An application can provide an intent to another application for it to call the application back when a certain condition is met, or a requested operation is completed. For example, when an application places a notification on the notification bar, it also provides an intent to the notification bar to call the application back when the user clicks that notification.

Ordinary intents cannot be used directly for this purpose, as they are executed based on the calling application's permissions. The Android framework provides a special intent type called android.app.PendingIntent.[7] This special intent type is executed based on the creating application's permissions instead of on the executing application's permissions. This makes it possible for applications to use pending intents as callback intents.

---

[7]http://developer.android.com/reference/android/app/PendingIntent.html.

Creating a Pending Intent

The PendingIntent class provides four static methods to create pending intents.

- getActivity is used for creating a pending intent to start an activity.

- getBroadcast is used for creating a pending intent to send a broadcast message.

- getService is used for creating a pending intent to start a service.

- getActivities is used for creating a pending intent to start multiple activities.

> **Note**   The getActivities method becomes very handy when starting the application from the notification bar, as it allows you to also rebuild the activity "back stack" and take the user to the detail activity.

You can use these methods to create a pending intent, as shown in Listing 3-7.

Listing 3-7. Creating an Intent to Launch the Contacts List

```
Intent intent = new Intent();
intent.setAction(Intent.ACTION_VIEW);
intent.setData(Uri.parse("content://contacts/people"));

PendingIntent pendingIntent = PendingIntent.getActivity(this, 0, intent, 0);
```

Once the pending intent is provided to the other application, the pending intent can be executed any time using its send() method, as shown in Listing 3-8.

Listing 3-8. Sending a Pending Intent

```
try {
  pendingIntent.send();
} catch (PendingIntent.CanceledException e) {
  e.printStackTrace();
}
```

Service

For longer-running operations, the lifespan of an activity may not be long enough for the task to complete. For example, if your application has to download a big video file from the Internet, you cannot expect the user to remain with that activity for the duration of the download operation. But as soon as the user walks away, the platform will terminate the activity without waiting for the operation to complete.

The Android framework provides an application component, known as android.app.Service,[8] to enable applications to perform longer-running operations in the background.

Services can be used both within the same application and also by other applications on the device if the service is exported.

Creating a Service

You can create a new service simply by deriving a new class from the android.app.Service class as shown in Listing 3-9.

Listing 3-9. Creating a New Android Service

```
package com.apress.helloworld;

import android.app.Service;
import android.content.Intent;
import android.os.IBinder;

public class MyService extends Service {
    @Override
    public IBinder onBind(Intent intent) {
        return null;
    }
}
```

As the onBind method is declared abstract in the Service class, you need to provide an implementation for it. For now you can safely ignore this detail, as you will learn more about it in the section "Binding to a Service."

---

[8]http://developer.android.com/reference/android/app/Service.html.

Declaring a Service

Creating a new service class does not automatically make the service available on the Android platform. The Android platform requires more meta information in order to make the service available. This meta information needs to be provided again as part of the Android manifest file through the `<service>`[9] XML tag, as shown in Listing 3-10.

Listing 3-10. Declaring the New Service in the `AndroidManifest.xml` File

```
<service
    android:name=".MyService"
    android:enabled="true"
    android:exported="false" >
</service>
```

Similar to the `<activity>` element, the `<service>` element can also contain `<intent-filter>` elements in its body to specify the actions that it can fulfill. If no intent filters are provided, the service can only be reached by explicitly specifying it as a component of the intent.

> **Caution**   The most important attribute of the `<service>` element is `android:exported`. It specifies whether the service can be accessed by other applications that are running on the device. By default, it is set to true for any services that specify any intent filters, meaning that it is available to other applications. To ensure the maximum security of your application, mark all internal services as not exported.

Restricting Access to a Service

If you prefer to export your services for other applications to use, the Android platform enables you to enforce access permissions for the service. By doing so, other applications will need to ask for that specific permission in their manifest file for the user to see and approve during the installation phase.

---

[9]http://developer.android.com/guide/topics/manifest/service-element.html.

As shown in Listing 3-11, in order to enforce a permission on a service, you need to

- Declare the permission using the `<permission>` tag in the manifest file of the application that will provide the service.

- Later mark the service to request this new permission by specifying it using the `android:permission` attribute of the `<service>` tag.

Listing 3-11. Declaring and Enforcing a Permission in the AndroidManifest.xml File

```xml
<?xml version="1.0" encoding="utf-8"?>
<manifest
    xmlns:android="http://schemas.android.com/apk/res/android"
    package="com.apress.helloworld" >

    <permission
        android:name="com.apress.permission.MY_SERVICE"
        android:protectionLevel="dangerous" />

    <application>

        ...

        <service
            android:name=".MyService"
            android:enabled="true"
            android:exported="true"
            android:permission=
        "com.apress.permission.MY_SERVICE">
        </service>
    </application>

</manifest>
```

Now that the service is exported by enforcing a permission, applications that would like to use this service must declare the permission in their manifest file, as shown in Listing 3-12.

Listing 3-12. Requesting the Permission in the AndroidManifest.xml File

```xml
<?xml version="1.0" encoding="utf-8"?>
<manifest
    xmlns:android="http://schemas.android.com/apk/res/android"
    package="com.apress.helloworld" >

    <uses-permission android:name=
            "com.apress.permission.MY_SERVICE" />

</manifest>
```

Service Life Cycle

As the user never directly interacts with the service, which is running in the background, its life cycle is slightly different than the activity life cycle. As visibility is not a concern for a service, the Service class provides fewer life cycle hooks. Figure 3-2 illustrates the flow between these life cycle states.

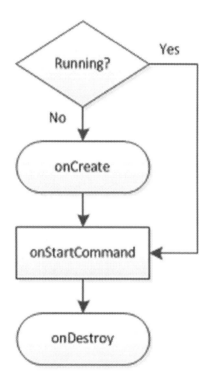

Figure 3-2. Service life cycle states

- onCreate is called when the service is first created.

- onStartCommand is called every time the service is explicitly started through an intent. While the service is running, this method can be called multiple times by the system to queue more work for the service.

- onDestroy is called when the service is no longer in use. The service should clean up any resources it holds.

Service Restart Strategy

As frequently indicated in this book, the Android platform will do whatever it takes to use system resources efficiently in order to provide a smooth user experience. For that reason, any application the user is not seeing or interacting with is treated as less important than the one in the foreground. When more resources are needed, the Android platform may decide to terminate the applications in memory by starting with the least important ones. A service that is running in the background is not considered as important, and it may be terminated by the platform at any given time.

The service start strategy can be adjusted through the return value of the onStartCommand method. The method can return one of the following constant values:

- START_FLAG_NOT_STICKY is returned if the service should be restarted after it has been killed by the platform unless an explicit start command is sent.

- START_FLAG_STICKY is returned if the service would like to be restarted after it has been killed by the platform. The original intent is not preserved.

- START_FLAG_REDELIVERY is returned if the service would like to be restarted and also needs the original intent to be redelivered.

Starting a Service

Depending on the use case, either the service can be started through an intent or the calling code can directly bind to the service.

Starting a Service with an Intent

The easiest way to start a service is through an intent. Application code can use the startService[10] method to start a service with a given intent, as shown in Listing 3-13.

Listing 3-13. Starting a Service with an Intent

```
Intent intent = new Intent(this, MyService.class);
startService(intent);
```

---

[10]http://developer.android.com/reference/android/content/Context.html#startService(android.content.Intent).

Intent Service

In order to facilitate this process, the Android framework provides the android.app.IntentService[11] class. A new class can be derived from the IntentService to handle the requested intents, as shown in Listing 3-14.

Listing 3-14. Intent Service to Process Requested Intents from a Queue

```
package com.apress.helloworld;

import android.app.IntentService;
import android.content.Intent;

public class MyService extends IntentService {
  public MyService() {
    super(MyService.class.getName());
  }

  @Override
  protected void onHandleIntent(Intent intent) {
    // handle intent
  }
}
```

Although this is the easiest way to start a service, the service and the calling code do not have any connection during the lifespan of the service.

Binding to a Service

If the calling code and the service will need to communicate throughout the lifespan of the service, then the service can be bounded, as shown in Listing 3-15.

Listing 3-15. Binding to a Service

```
package com.apress.helloworld;

import android.app.Activity;
import android.content.ComponentName;
import android.content.Context;
import android.content.Intent;
import android.content.ServiceConnection;
import android.os.Bundle;
import android.os.IBinder;
```

---

[11]http://developer.android.com/reference/android/app/IntentService.html.

```
public class MyActivity extends Activity {
  private IBinder service;

  @Override
  protected void onCreate(Bundle savedInstanceState) {
    ...

  bindService(new Intent(this, MyService.class),
  new ServiceConnection() {
  @Override
  public void onServiceConnected(
  ComponentName componentName, IBinder iBinder) {
  // service connected
  service = iBinder;
  }

  @Override
  public void onServiceDisconnected(
  ComponentName componentName) {
  // service disconnected
  }
  },
  Context.BIND_AUTO_CREATE);
    }
}
```

As mentioned earlier in the "Declaring a Service" section, services can be either local to the current application or used remotely from another application that is exporting the service. The communication channel between the calling code and the service heavily depends on this. According to service type, the onBind method of the service should return the proper binder service channel.

Local Service

In the case of a local service, the communication channel can easily be provided by deriving a new class from the android.os.Binder[12] class and returning the service instance directly as shown in Listing 3-16.

---

[12]http://developer.android.com/reference/android/os/Binder.html.

Listing 3-16. Local Binder Implementation for Locally Used Services

```
package com.apress.helloworld;

import android.app.Service;
import android.content.Intent;
import android.os.Binder;
import android.os.IBinder;

public class MyService extends Service {
  public class LocalBinder extends Binder {
  MyService getService() {
  return MyService.this;
  }
  }

  private final LocalBinder localBinder = new LocalBinder();

  @Override
  public IBinder onBind(Intent intent) {
    return localBinder;
  }
}
```

The calling code can extract the service instance from the binder and use it directly as shown in Listing 3-17.

Listing 3-17. Getting the Service Instance from the Binder

```
@Override
public void onServiceConnected(ComponentName componentName,
                               IBinder iBinder) {
  // service connected
  MyService.LocalBinder localBinder =
        (MyService.LocalBinder) iBinder;

  MyService service = localBinder.getService();
}
```

Remote Service

In the case of remotely used services, as the calling application and the service reside in two different processes, the communication gets carried through the binder via IPC (inter-process communication). Depending on the purpose of the service, either a service interface can be defined using Android Interface Definition Language (AIDL) or a simple message queue can be used to carry primitive data types between the two processes.

Communicating Using AIDL

Using AIDL, an interface for the service must be defined, as shown in Listing 3-18.

Listing 3-18. IMyServiceInterface.aidl Interface File

```
package com.apress.helloworld;

interface IMyServiceInterface {
    int add(int a, int b);
}
```

During the compilation phase, a set of class files will be automatically generated from this AIDL interface file. Both the service and the calling code will need these class files to communicate through the binder channel.

The service needs to implement the generated stub class in order to provide the implementation for the interface methods, as showing in Listing 3-19.

Listing 3-19. MyService Implementing the Stub Interface

```
package com.apress.helloworld;

import android.app.Service;
import android.content.Intent;
import android.os.IBinder;
import android.os.RemoteException;

public class MyService extends Service {
  private final IMyServiceInterface.Stub serviceBinder =
        new IMyServiceInterface.Stub() {
    @Override
    public int add(int a, int b) throws RemoteException {
      return a + b;
    }
  };

  @Override
  public IBinder onBind(Intent intent) {
    return serviceBinder;
  }
}
```

In the same way, the calling code should also use the generated interface class to communicate with the service, as shown in Listing 3-20.

Listing 3-20. Calling Code Using the Interface to Communicate with the Service

```java
package com.apress.helloworld;

import android.app.Activity;
import android.content.ComponentName;
import android.content.Context;
import android.content.Intent;
import android.content.ServiceConnection;
import android.os.Bundle;
import android.os.IBinder;
import android.os.RemoteException;

public class MyActivity extends Activity {
  private IMyServiceInterface myServiceInterface;

  @Override
  protected void onCreate(Bundle savedInstanceState) {
    super.onCreate(savedInstanceState);
    setContentView(R.layout.activity_my);

    Intent intent = new Intent();
    intent.setComponent(new ComponentName(
        "com.apress.helloworld",
        "com.apress.helloworld.MyService"));

    bindService(intent, new ServiceConnection() {
        @Override
        public void onServiceConnected(
            ComponentName componentName, IBinder iBinder) {
          // service connected
          myServiceInterface =
              IMyServiceInterface.Stub.asInterface(iBinder);

          try {
            int total = myServiceInterface.add(10, 20);

          } catch (RemoteException e) {
            e.printStackTrace();
          }
        }
```

```
        @Override
        public void onServiceDisconnected(
            ComponentName componentName) {
          // service disconnected
          myServiceInterface = null;
        }
      },
      Context.BIND_AUTO_CREATE);
  }
}
```

Although it requires more work, using AIDL enables you to define a clear interface between the service and the code that will interact with the interface remotely.

Communication Using Message Queue

In certain situations, the communication requirement between the service and the calling code could be very minimal. In such cases, using AIDL could be seen as overkill. The Android framework provides the `android.os.Messenger`[13] class to furnish a simple message queue between the service and the calling code. The message queue carries primitive data types, and it does not require any custom interfaces.

In order to use the `Messenger`, the service needs to implement a message queue, as shown in Listing 3-21.

Listing 3-21. Service to Process Request Received Through Messages

```
package com.apress.helloworld;

import android.app.Service;
import android.content.Intent;
import android.os.Handler;
import android.os.IBinder;
import android.os.Message;
import android.os.Messenger;

public class MyService extends Service {
  public static final int MESSAGE_DOWNLOAD = 1;
```

---

[13]http://developer.android.com/reference/android/os/Messenger.html

```
private class RequestHandler extends Handler {
  @Override
  public void handleMessage(Message msg) {
    switch (msg.what) {
      case MESSAGE_DOWNLOAD:
        // start downloading
        break;

      default:
        super.handleMessage(msg);
    }
  }
}

private final Messenger messenger =
new Messenger(new RequestHandler());

  @Override
  public IBinder onBind(Intent intent) {
    return messenger.getBinder();
  }
}
```

This message queue receives android.os.Message[14] instances and processes them as they come in. In order to send these messages, the calling code also relies on a Messenger instance, as shown in Listing 3-22.

Listing 3-22. Activity Communicating with the Service by Sending Messages

```
package com.apress.helloworld;

import android.app.Activity;
import android.content.ComponentName;
import android.content.Context;
import android.content.Intent;
import android.content.ServiceConnection;
import android.os.Bundle;
import android.os.IBinder;
import android.os.Message;
import android.os.Messenger;
import android.os.RemoteException;
```

---

[14]http://developer.android.com/reference/android/os/Message.html.

```java
public class MyActivity extends Activity {
  public static final int MESSAGE_DOWNLOAD = 1;

  @Override
  protected void onCreate(Bundle savedInstanceState) {
    super.onCreate(savedInstanceState);
    setContentView(R.layout.activity_my);

    Intent intent = new Intent();
    intent.setComponent(new ComponentName(
        "com.apress.helloworld",
        "com.apress.helloworld.MyService"));

    bindService(intent, new ServiceConnection() {
      @Override
      public void onServiceConnected(
          ComponentName componentName, IBinder iBinder) {
        Messenger service = new Messenger(iBinder);

Message downloadMessage = Message.obtain(
null, MESSAGE_DOWNLOAD);

try {
service.send(downloadMessage);
} catch (RemoteException e) {
e.printStackTrace();
}
      }

      @Override
      public void onServiceDisconnected(
          ComponentName componentName) {

      }
    }, Context.BIND_AUTO_CREATE);
  }
}
```

System Services

The Android platform itself also exposes various device and platform features as services. Compared to the services that applications provide, the Android framework makes it much easier to consume these services by providing classes as part of its application programming interfaces (APIs). Applications can interact with these services using these existing interfaces without dealing with intents, AIDL, and binding.

The platform service interfaces can be obtained through the getSystemService[15] method of the current context by simply passing the name of the service using one of the defined constant values in the context class, as shown in Listing 3-23.

Listing 3-23. Getting the Power Service Interface from the Current Context

```
PowerManager powerManager =
        (PowerManager) getSystemService(POWER_SERVICE);
```

Following is list of notable services that are exposed by the Android platform:

- android.app.ActivityManager[16] enables you to interact with global activity state of the system, such as getting the recent activity with which the user was interacting.

- android.os.PowerManager[17] enables you to control the device's power configuration (e.g., preventing the device from going into sleep mode).

- android.app.AlarmManager[18] allows the application to schedule a pending intent for execution at a later time, even when the requesting application is not running.

- android.app.NotificationManager[19] allows the application to inform the user regarding background events by displaying notifications on the notification bar.

- android.location.LocationManager[20] allows the application to receive location information from the device's location sources (e.g., the GPS).

- android.app.DownloadManager[21] allows the application to request long-running HTTP downloads. The download service handles the download in the background and informs the system when the download is terminated.

---

[15]http://developer.android.com/reference/android/content/Context.html#getSystemService(java.lang.String).
[16]http://developer.android.com/reference/android/app/Activity Manager.html.
[17]http://developer.android.com/reference/android/os/PowerManager.html.
[18]http://developer.android.com/reference/android/app/AlarmManager.html.
[19]http://developer.android.com/reference/android/app/NotificationManager.html.
[20]http://developer.android.com/reference/android/location/LocationManager.html.
[21]http://developer.android.com/reference/android/app/DownloadManager.html.

▓ android.net.ConnectivityManager[22] allows the application to query the connectivity state of the device (e.g., cellular or WiFi connectivity).

▓ android.net.wifi.WifiManager[23] allows the application to interact with the WiFi network (e.g., searching for WiFi networks and adding new WiFi network configurations).

▓ android.app.UiModeManager[24] allows the application to query and manipulate the device's UI mode (e.g., switching between car mode and normal mode).

▓ android.view.inputmethod.InputMethodManager[25] allows the application to control the input methods (e.g., displaying and hiding the soft input window).

▓ android.app.KeyguardManager[26] allows the application to lock and unlock the key guard screen.

▓ android.app.SearchManager[27] provides access to platform search functionality.

▓ android.view.WindowManager[28] provides access to a top-level window manager to enable you to place custom windows.

▓ android.view.LayoutInflater[29] allows you to inflate layout resources from a given resource in the context.

▓ android.os.Vibrator[30] allows the application to control the vibrator on the device to notify the user in silent mode.

---

[22]http://developer.android.com/reference/android/net/ConnectivityManager.html.
[23]http://developer.android.com/reference/android/net/wifi/WifiManager.html.
[24]http://developer.android.com/reference/android/app/UiModeManager.html.
[25]http://developer.android.com/reference/android/view/inputmethod/
InputMethodManager.html.
[26]http://developer.android.com/reference/android/app/KeyguardManager.html.
[27]http://developer.android.com/reference/android/app/SearchManager.html.
[28]http://developer.android.com/reference/android/view/WindowManager.html.
[29]http://developer.android.com/reference/android/view/LayoutInflater.html.
[30]http://developer.android.com/reference/android/os/Vibrator.html.

> **Caution**   Most of these services require the calling application to have certain permissions. Before using any of these platform services, make sure to have these permissions listed in your application's manifest.

Content Provider

As mentioned earlier in the "Service" section, both activities and services can be exported so that other applications that are running on the same device can blend them into their work flows. Although accessing parts of other applications are very useful, in certain cases, you would simply need access to the application's data rather than its activities and services.

The Android platform provides an application component, known as the content provider, that manages access to a structured set of data. It is a standard interface that connects the data of one application with the code running on another application. The content provider achieves this by providing proper data encapsulation and also security. The content provider and the data it contains are referred through content URIs, such as the following:

```
content://com.apress.booksprovider/books/1.
```

Creating a Content Provider

A new content provider can be created simply by deriving a new class from the android.content.ContentProvider[31] class. As shown in Listing 3-24, the abstract ContentProvider class has six abstract methods that need to be implemented.

- ▓ query method is called to query the provider for data.
- ▓ insert method is called to insert new content into the provider.
- ▓ update method is called to update the content in the provider with new content.
- ▓ delete method is called to delete content from the provider.

---

[31]http://developer.android.com/reference/android/content/ContentProvider.html.

■ getType method is called to get the MIME type for content that will be returned for the given URI.

■ onCreate method is called by the platform when the content provider gets instantiated. This method gets called before any other method.

> **Caution**   All of these methods, except the onCreate method, can be called multiple times from different threads. For that reason, their implementation should be thread safe.

Listing 3-24. Book Content Provider Implementation

```
package com.apress.bookprovider;

import android.content.ContentProvider;
import android.content.ContentValues;
import android.content.UriMatcher;
import android.database.Cursor;
import android.database.MatrixCursor;
import android.net.Uri;

public class BookProvider extends ContentProvider {
  private static final int QUERY_ALL_BOOKS = 1;
  private static final int QUERY_BY_BOOK_ID = 2;

  private static final UriMatcher URI_MATCHER =
          new UriMatcher(UriMatcher.NO_MATCH);

  static {
    URI_MATCHER.addURI(BookContract.AUTHORITY,
        BookContract.CONTENT_PATH, QUERY_ALL_BOOKS);

    URI_MATCHER.addURI(BookContract.AUTHORITY,
        BookContract.CONTENT_PATH + "/#", QUERY_BY_BOOK_ID);
  }

  @Override
  public boolean onCreate() {
    return false;
  }
```

```java
@Override
public Cursor query(Uri uri, String[] projection,
    String selection, String[] selectionArgs,
    String sortOrder) {

  MatrixCursor matrixCursor = new MatrixCursor(new String[]{
      BookContract.BookColumns._ID,
      BookContract.BookColumns.BOOK_NAME,
      BookContract.BookColumns.BOOK_ISBN
  });

  matrixCursor.addRow(new Object[]{
      1,
      "Android Apps",
      "978-1430244349"
  });

  return matrixCursor;
}

@Override
public Uri insert(Uri uri, ContentValues values) {
  return null;
}

@Override
public int update(Uri uri, ContentValues values,
  String selection, String[] selectionArgs) {
  return 0;
}

@Override
public int delete(Uri uri, String selection,
    String[] selectionArgs) {
  return 0;
}

@Override
public String getType(Uri uri) {
  switch (URI_MATCHER.match(uri)) {
    case QUERY_ALL_BOOKS:
      return BookContract.CONTENT_TYPE;

    case QUERY_BY_BOOK_ID:
      return BookContract.CONTENT_ITEM_TYPE;

    default:
      return null;
  }
}
}
```

Content Provider Contract

The content provider contract class defines constants that help applications to work with the content URIs, column names, and other features of a content provider. Contract classes are not automatically generated. The application developer is expected to generate them as a best practice, as shown in Listing 3-25.

Listing 3-25. Book Content Provider Contract

```
package com.apress.bookprovider;

import android.net.Uri;
import android.provider.BaseColumns;

public interface BookContract {
  String AUTHORITY = "com.apress.bookprovider";

  Uri AUTHORITY_URI = Uri.parse("content://" + AUTHORITY);

  String CONTENT_PATH = "books";

  Uri CONTENT_URI = Uri.withAppendedPath(
          AUTHORITY_URI, CONTENT_PATH);

  String CONTENT_TYPE =
    "vnd.android.cursor.dir/vnd.com.apress.bookprovider.book";

  String CONTENT_ITEM_TYPE =
    "vnd.android.cursor.item/vnd.com.apress.bookprovider.book";

  interface BookColumns extends BaseColumns {
    String BOOK_NAME = "book_name";
    String BOOK_ISBN = "book_isbn";
  }
}
```

Declaring a Content Provider

Like the activities and the services, content providers are not exposed until they get properly declared in the application's manifest file. The `<provider>`[32] XML tag is used to declare a content provider as shown in Listing 3-26.

---

[32]http://developer.android.com/guide/topics/manifest/provider-element.html.

Listing 3-26. Declaring Book Content Provider in the AndroidManifest.xml File

```
<?xml version="1.0" encoding="utf-8"?>
<manifest
  xmlns:android="http://schemas.android.com/apk/res/android"
  package="com.apress.bookprovider">

  <application>
    ...

  <provider
  android:name=".BookProvider"
  android:authorities="com.apress.bookprovider"
  android:enabled="true"
  android:exported="true"></provider>
  </application>
</manifest>
```

The most important attribute of the `<provider>` tag is the
`android:authorities` attribute. It defines the unique name of this content
provider. By convention, content providers should be named by having the
application package as the prefix, such as `com.apress.bookprovider`. The
Android platform stores a reference to the content provider according to this
authority name. This authority name is also used as part of the URI by other
applications to access the content provider.

```
content://<authority>/<path>/<id>
content://com.apress.bookprovider/book/1
```

Content Provider Security

Content providers can also declare two separate permissions for both
reading and writing. The read permission is specified through the
`android:readPermission` attribute; only applications with the proper
permission can call the query method of this content provider. Likewise,
the write permission is specified through the `android:writePermission`
attribute, and only applications with the proper permission can call the
insert, update, and delete methods. If two separate permissions are not
needed, the `android:permission` attribute can be used to specify only one
permission to access the content provider—the same as for other Android
components.

Accessing a Content Provider

Content providers can be accessed through the android.content.
ContentResolver[33] class. An instance of ContentResolver class can be
obtained by calling the getContentResolver method of the current context,
as shown in Listing 3-27.

Listing 3-27. Getting Data from Content Provider Through Content Resolver

```
Cursor cursor = getContentResolver().query(
    BookContract.CONTENT_URI,
    null,
    null,
    null,
    null);

if (cursor != null) {
  try {
    if (cursor.moveToFirst()) {
      int bookNameColumn = cursor.getColumnIndexOrThrow(
          BookContract.BookColumns.BOOK_NAME);

      int bookIsbnColumn = cursor.getColumnIndexOrThrow(
          BookContract.BookColumns.BOOK_ISBN);

      do {
        String bookName = cursor.getString(bookNameColumn);
        String bookIsbn = cursor.getString(bookIsbnColumn);

      } while (cursor.moveToNext());
    }
  } finally {
    cursor.close();
  }
}
```

---

[33]http://developer.android.com/reference/android/content/ContentResolver.html.

System Content Providers

Just as system services do, the Android platform also provides a set of content providers to enable the application to access the user's information. Following is a list of the most notable content providers that the platform provides:

- **Alarm Clock Provider**[34] provides access to the user's alarms and also enables the application to manipulate its existing alarms.

- **Browser Provider**[35] allows access to the user's bookmarks and history.

- **Calendar Provider**[36] allows access to the user's calendar, and enables the application to manipulate it.

- **Contacts Provider**[37] allows access to the user's contact list.

- **Call Log Provider**[38] provides access to the received and placed calls.

- **Document Provider**[39] provides a generic interface to access the user's documents across all document storage providers, such as documents kept at cloud storage services.

- **Media Store Provider**[40] provides access to meta data for all media files that are available on the device, such as music, video, and photos.

- **Settings Provider**[41] provides access to global system-level device preferences.

- **Telephony Provider**[42] provides access to telephony data, such as SMS (Short Message Service) and MMS (Multimedia Messaging Service) messages and the APN (Access Point Name) list.

---

[34]http://developer.android.com/reference/android/provider/AlarmClock.html.

[35]http://developer.android.com/reference/android/provider/Browser.html.

[36]http://developer.android.com/guide/topics/providers/calendar-provider.html.

[37]http://developer.android.com/guide/topics/providers/contacts-provider.html.

[38]http://developer.android.com/reference/android/provider/CallLog.html.

[39]http://developer.android.com/guide/topics/providers/document-provider.html.

[40]http://developer.android.com/reference/android/provider/MediaStore.html.

[41]http://developer.android.com/reference/android/provider/Settings.html.

[42]http://developer.android.com/reference/android/provider/Telephony.html.

- **User Dictionary Provider**[43] provides access to user-defined words for input methods to use for predictive text input.

- **Voicemail Provider**[44] provides access to the user's voicemails.

Broadcast Messages

The Android platform provides a system-wide message bus facility called broadcast messages. This facility enables applications and the system to propagate events and state change information to the interested parties by broadcasting an intent as a message.

Sending a Broadcast Message

A broadcast message can be sent through the sendBroadcast[45] method of the current context.

As shown in Listing 3-28, the sendBroadcast method takes an intent as the message.

Listing 3-28. Sending Broadcast Messages

```
Intent intent = new Intent();
intent.setAction("com.apress.bookreceiver.action.BOOK_NEW");
intent.addCategory(Intent.CATEGORY_DEFAULT);
intent.setData(Uri.parse(
        "http://www.apress.com/9781430248279"));

sendBroadcast(intent);
```

> **Tip**   If you are only sending the broadcast messages to the internal components of your application, you should use the LocalBroadcastManager's[46] sendBroadcast() method instead in order to optimize the delivery and to ensure the security of your messages.

---

[43]http://developer.android.com/reference/android/provider/CallLog.html.
[44]http://developer.android.com/reference/android/provider/VoicemailContract.html.
[45]http://developer.android.com/reference/android/content/Context.html#sendBroadcast.
[46]http://developer.android.com/reference/android/support/v4/content/LocalBroadcastManager.html.

Receiving the Broadcast Message

In order to receive the broadcast message, the application should derive a new class from the `android.content.BroadcastReceiver`[47] class, as shown in Listing 3-29.

Listing 3-29. Broadcast Receiver Class Implementation

```
package com.apress.bookreceiver;

import android.content.BroadcastReceiver;
import android.content.Context;
import android.content.Intent;

public class BookBroadcastReceiver extends BroadcastReceiver {
  @Override
  public void onReceive(Context context, Intent intent) {
  }
}
```

Simply deriving the class is not sufficient to receive the broadcast messages. The application can inform the Android platform regarding its interest in receiving broadcast messages by registering either through the manifest file or dynamically through the code.

Registering for Broadcast Messages Through the Manifest

The `<receiver>`[48] XML tag is used to register the broadcast receiver in the application's manifest, as shown in Listing 3-30.

Listing 3-30. Registering the Broadcast Receiver Through the AndroidManifest.xml File

```
<?xml version="1.0" encoding="utf-8"?>
<manifest xmlns:android="http://schemas.android.com/apk/res/android"
  package="com.apress.bookreceiver">

  <receiver
  android:name=".BookBroadcastReceiver"
```

[47]http://developer.android.com/reference/android/content/Broadcast Receiver.html.
[48]http://developer.android.com/guide/topics/manifest/receiver-element.html.

```
android:enabled="true"
android:exported="true">
<intent-filter>
<action android:name=
"com.apress.bookreceiver.action.BOOK_NEW" />
<category android:name=
"android.intent.category.DEFAULT" />
</intent-filter>
</receiver>
 </application>

</manifest>
```

Registering for Broadcast Messages Through the Code

The broadcast receiver can also be dynamically registered through the registerReceiver[49] method of the current context, as shown in Listing 3-31.

Listing 3-31. Registering the Broadcast Receiver Through the Code

```
BookBroadcastReceiver bookBroadcastReceiver = new BookBroadcastReceiver();

IntentFilter intentFilter = new IntentFilter();
intentFilter.addAction(
    "com.apress.bookreceiver.action.BOOK_NEW");
intentFilter.addCategory(Intent.CATEGORY_DEFAULT);

registerReceiver(bookBroadcastReceiver, intentFilter);
```

Broadcast Receiver Life Cycle

The application running the broadcast receiver is only alive during the duration of onReceive method of the broadcast receiver. Once the onReceive method returns, the platform considers the application finished. If the processing of the message requires a longer time, the broadcast receiver should start a service to process the message in the background.

---

[49]http://developer.android.com/reference/android/content/Context.html#
registerReceiver(android.content.BroadcastReceiver,android.content.IntentFilter).

Broadcast Receiver Security

Using the same security components that are used to secure the activity and the services, applications can enforce permissions on both the broadcasted messages and the broadcast receiver.

Context

The context is an Android component that provides an interface to the global information about the application environment. Both Activity and Service classes are derived from the android.content.Context[50] class, and they can act as the context for other parts of the application. The context provides an interface to access the application resources, including the features such as start activities and services. The startActivity and startService methods that you have learned about in this section are actually part of the Context class. The lifespan of a context is defined by the type of class that is acting as the context. For example, if the context is provided through an instance of the Activity class, its lifespan is the same as the activity's lifespan. Once the activity is destroyed, the instance can no longer provide context-specific features.

Application

As both the activity and service lifespans are limited, they are not good candidates for keeping the global state of an application. The Android framework provides the android.app.Application[51] class for that purpose. The lifespan of the Application class lasts from the time the application is started until the time the application is terminated by the platform.

The Application class itself does not provide any mechanism to store additional information; however, a new class can be derived from the Application class to provide that functionality, as shown in Listing 3-32.

Listing 3-32. New Application Class to Hold Global Values

```
package com.apress.helloworld;

import android.app.Application;
```

[50]http://developer.android.com/reference/android/content/Context.html.
[51]http://developer.android.com/reference/android/app/Application.html.

```
public class MyApplication extends Application {
  private String globalValue;

  public String getGlobalValue() {
    return globalValue;
  }

  public void setGlobalValue(String globalValue) {
    this.globalValue = globalValue;
  }
}
```

For the application to use this new Application class, it needs to be declared in the application manifest through the <application>[52] XML tag with the android:name attribute, as shown in Listing 3-33.

Listing 3-33. Declaring the New Application in the AndroidManifest.xml File

```
<?xml version="1.0" encoding="utf-8"?>
<manifest
    xmlns:android="http://schemas.android.com/apk/res/android"
    package="com.apress.helloworld">

  <application
    android:name=".MyApplication"

    ...
    >

  </application>
</manifest>
```

This instance can be accessed through the getApplication() method, as shown in Listing 3-34.

Listing 3-34. Getting the Application Instance

```
MyApplication myApplication = (MyApplication) getApplication();
myApplication.setGlobalValue("1234");
```

---

[52]http://developer.android.com/guide/topics/manifest/application-element.html.

Just as the Activity class does, the Application class also provides hooks to the application life cycle changes. The platform calls the onCreate method of the Application class when the application is first initialized, and later it calls the onDestroy method when the application is being terminated. The application can override these hooks to properly initialize itself and also to release any resources that it holds while the application is terminating.

Summary

In this section you have learned about the fundamental components that the Android framework provides, such as activities, services, and content providers. Knowing how to use these components properly is the key for developing successful Android applications. In the next chapter, you will be learning about the UI components that the Android framework provides.

Chapter **4**

Application Resources

Resources are one of the most important components of an application. It is always good practice to externalize resources in order to maintain consistency and to prevent resource duplication, as resources can be referenced from multiple places within the application. Decoupling the code and the resources also has other advantages.

- **Localization of the Application:** The application can carry an alternative set of resources for various languages, and it can switch between them based on the user's locale during runtime. This makes it possible to support multiple languages and locales with a single application binary.

- **Device Specific Look and Feel:** As the Android platform is highly fragmented, there is no magic user interface (UI) configuration that will look and feel the same on all Android devices. The screen layouts and also the images mostly need to be customized based on screen size and screen density. Externalization of resources enables the application to use the proper resource set based on the device's specifications.

The Android framework provides a comprehensive set of application programming interfaces (APIs) and a structure to organize resources in order to seamlessly pick the proper resources on behalf of the application based on the characteristics of the runtime environment.

In the following section, I detail how to structure your resources, and how to access them from within your application through the APIs.

Structure of Resources

The Android Software Development Kit (SDK) requires the application resources to be placed in a specific subdirectory of the src/main/res directory. As shown in Listing 4-1, the example application has an image resource called icon.png, which is placed in the drawable subdirectory, a screen layout called main.xml in the layout subdirectory, and some string resources in the values subdirectory as a strings.xml file.

Listing 4-1. Structure of Application Resources

```
Hello Android
    |
    `- src
        `- main
            `- res
                |- drawable
                |     `- icon.png
                |
                |- layout
                |     `- main.xml
                |
                `- values
                      `- strings.xml
```

The names of the resource subdirectories are important. The Android framework cannot find the resources if they are not properly placed.

Android Studio does not automatically create all possible resource subdirectories. You can create the missing ones as you need them at any time, by right-clicking the res directory and choosing New ➤ Android Resource Directory from the context menu to launch the *New Resource Directory* dialog as shown in Figure 4-1.

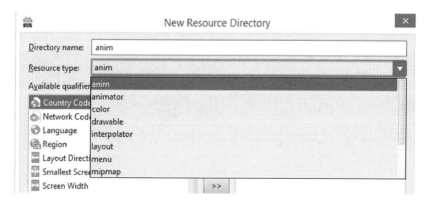

Figure 4-1. New resource directory dialog

Resource Groups

Android groups the resources under nine main categories based on their type. Each of these nine resources groups has its individual subdirectories within the `src/res` resource directory. Once you compile and build the application, the Android toolchain autogenerates a Java class file `<application package name>.R` (i.e., `com.apress.R`), to provide access to these resources from the application code. Table 4-1 lists these nine resource groups, their corresponding resource subdirectories, and their groups within the R constants class.

Table 4-1. Resource Groups, Their Subdirectories, Their R Constants, and XML Prefixes

Resource Group	Subdirectory	Reference in Code	Reference in XML
Property Animations	animator	R.animator	@animator/<file>
Tween Animations	anim	R.anim	@anim/<file>
Color State List	color	R.color	@color/<file>
Drawables	drawable	R.drawable	@drawable/<file>
Layouts	layout	R.layout	@layout/<file>
Menu	menu	R.menu	@menu/<file>
Raw	raw	R.raw	
Simple Values	values	R.arrays	@bool/<id>
		R.bool	@color/<id>
		R.color	@dimen/<id>
		R.dimen	@integer/<id>
		R.integer	@string/<id>
		R.string	@style/<id>
		R.style	
XML	xml	R.xml	

> **Caution** If you are unable to find your resources in the R class, please make sure that the correct R class is imported in your source file. Android framework resources are also provided through the android.R class, and this may have been unintentionally imported by the Android Studio IDE.

Property Animation Resources

The *property animation*[1] resource describes the steps to animate any object on the screen by changing its properties at certain intervals during a defined time window. As shown in Listing 4-2, these resources are provided as XML files. Android expects them to be placed in the src/res/animator directory.

Listing 4-2. src/res/animator/example.xml Property Animation Resource File

```
<?xml version="1.0" encoding="utf-8"?>
<set xmlns:android=
    "http://schemas.android.com/apk/res/android">
    <objectAnimator android:propertyName="x"
        android:duration="1000"
        android:valueFrom="10"
        android:valueTo="100"
        android:valueType="intType" />
</set>
```

Once they are declared, the animation resources can be accessed through the R.animator.<resource file name>, as shown in Listing 4-3. The name of the resource file is used as the resource ID.

Listing 4-3. Using the Animation Resource from the Code

```
AnimatorSet animatorSet = (AnimatorSet) AnimatorInflater.loadAnimator(
        this, R.animator.example);
```

---

[1]http://developer.android.com/guide/topics/graphics/prop-animation.html.

Tween Animation Resources

The *tween animation*[2] resource describes the steps to animate an object on the screen by applying a series of simple transformations to its content. As shown in Listing 4-4, the src/res/anim directory also provides these resources as XML files. The name of the resource file is used as the resource ID.

Listing 4-4. src/res/anim/twin.xml Tween Animation Resource File

```xml
<?xml version="1.0" encoding="utf-8"?>
<set xmlns:android=
    "http://schemas.android.com/apk/res/android">
    <scale android:fromXScale="1.0"
        android:toXScale="2.0"
        android:duration="1000" />
    <rotate android:fromDegrees="0"
        android:toDegrees="180"
        android:duration="1000" />
</set>
```

The tween animation resource can later be accessed through the R.anim.<resource file name>, as shown in Listing 4-5.

Listing 4-5. Using the Tween Animation Resource from the Code

```java
TextView textView = (TextView) findViewById(R.id.hello_world);
Animation animation = AnimationUtils.loadAnimation(
        this, R.anim.tween);
textView.startAnimation(animation);
```

Color State List Resources

The *color state list*[3] resource describes the colors for different states of a view. For example, a different set of colors could be applied for each state of a button. As shown in Listing 4-6, the src/res/color directory provides these resources as XML files. The name of the resource file is used as the resource ID.

---

[2]http://developer.android.com/guide/topics/graphics/view-animation.
html#tween-animation.

[3]http://developer.android.com/guide/topics/resources/color-list-resource.html.

Listing 4-6. src/res/color/button.xml Color State List Resource File

```xml
<?xml version="1.0" encoding="utf-8"?>
<selector xmlns:android="http://schemas.android.com/apk/res/android">
    <item android:color="#ffff0000"
        android:state_pressed="true" />
    <item android:color="#ff00ff00"
        android:state_focused="true" />
    <item android:color="#ff0000ff" />
</selector>
```

The color state list resource can then be accessed within the code through the R.color.<resource file name> as shown in Listing 4-7. In the next chapter, I will show you how to reference to the color state list resource directly from the layouts.

Listing 4-7. Using the Color State List Resource from the Code

```
ColorStateList colorStateList =
        getResources().getColorStateList(R.color.button);
```

Drawable Resources

The drawable resources are graphics that can be drawn to the screen. You can reference the drawable resources from the application code using the Resources.getDrawable method and by providing their unique resource ID through the R.drawable.<resource name> constants.Android supports several types of drawables.

Bitmap File

A bitmap file is an image file in PNG, JPEG, or GIF format. You can obtain a drawable resource from these image files by simply placing them into the src/res/drawable directory. The name of the image file acts as the unique resource ID for the drawable resource.

XML Bitmap File

You can apply additional attributes to an existing bitmap file by using an XML bitmap file. It is an XML file that points to an existing bitmap file and declares the additional attributes such as anti-aliasing and dithering using the <bitmap>[4] XML tag, as shown in Listing 4-8.

---

[4]http://developer.android.com/guide/topics/resources/drawable-resource.html#bitmap-element.

Listing 4-8. src/res/drawable/antialias.xml XML Bitmap File Drawable Resource File

```
<?xml version="1.0" encoding="utf-8"?>
<bitmap xmlns:android="http://schemas.android.com/apk/res/android"
    android:src="@drawable/ic_launcher"
    android:antialias="true" />
```

Nine-Patch File

The nine-patch file is a stretchable bitmap file that Android will automatically scale to accommodate the size of the view in which the drawable is placed as the background. Nine-patch files are also expected to be placed in the src/res/drawable directory. For Android to be able to distinguish between the ordinary bitmap files and the nine-patch files, the files are expected to have .9 extension between the file name and the extension, such as button.9.png.

Nine-patch files do not scale entirely as do the ordinary bitmap files. They carry additional information about the stretchable areas, as shown in Figure 4-2.

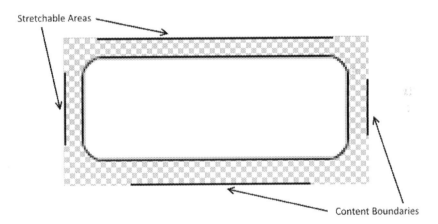

Figure 4-2. Border marks of a nine-patch file

- The left and top border lines define which pixels of the bitmap are allowed to stretch.

- The right and bottom border lines define the boundary of the area in which the contents are allowed to lie.

In order to make it easier to generate nine-patch files from the existing bitmap files, the Android SDK comes with a tool called *Draw 9 Patch*. It can be found in the <Android SDK>/tools directory as draw9patch.bat or draw9patch.sh, depending on the operating system.

XML Nine-Patch File

As does the XML bitmap file, the XML nine-patch file simply refers to an existing nine-patch and provides additional parameters, such as dithering, using the <nine-patch>[5] XML tag as shown in Listing 4-9.

Listing 4-9. XML Nine-Patch File Applying Dithering to the Existing Nine-Patch

```
<?xml version="1.0" encoding="utf-8"?>
<nine-patch
    xmlns:android="http://schemas.android.com/apk/res/android"
    android:src="@drawable/button"
    android:dither="true" />
```

Shape Drawable

Shape drawable is a generic shape that is defined in XML format using the <shape>[6] XML tag. The shape drawable supports all basic shapes—such as rectangle, oval, line, and ring. You can also apply corners, gradients, and colors to the shape objects through the XML resource file using the appropriate tags, as shown in Listing 4-10.

Listing 4-10. src/res/drawable/shape.xml Shape Resource File

```
<?xml version="1.0" encoding="utf-8"?>
<shape xmlns:android=
    "http://schemas.android.com/apk/res/android"
    android:shape="rectangle">

    <corners android:radius="4dp" />

    <gradient
        android:startColor="#FF00"
        android:endColor="#F0F0"
        android:angle="20"/>

    <padding android:left="4dp"
        android:top="4dp"
        android:right="4dp"
        android:bottom="4dp" />
</shape>
```

---

[5]http://developer.android.com/guide/topics/resources/drawable-resource.html#ninepatch-element.
[6]http://developer.android.com/guide/topics/resources/drawable-resource.html#shape-element.

You can then reference and apply the shape object as any other ordinary drawable resource.

State List

The state list drawable is a group of several images that are mapped to different states of an object. Based on the current state of the object, Android uses the correct image from the provided list. For example, using the state list drawable, you can provide different images for each state of a button. You can define the state list drawable in XML format using the <selector> XML tag with nested <item> XML tags representing each image, as shown in Listing 4-11.

Listing 4-11. State List Drawable for Different States of a Button

```xml
<?xml version="1.0" encoding="utf-8"?>
<selector xmlns:android="http://schemas.android.com/apk/res/android">
    <item android:drawable="@drawable/button_pressed "
        android:state_pressed="true" />

    <item android:drawable="@drawable/button_focused "
        android:state_focused="true" />
</selector>
```

Layout Resources

The layout resource file defines the architecture of the UI. It consists of the list of view components and attributes defining how they should be placed on the screen. As shown in Listing 4-8, the src/res/layout directory also provides these resources as XML files. The name of the layout resource file is used as the resource ID.

Listing 4-12. src/res/layout/activity_my.xml Layout Resource File

```xml
<RelativeLayout xmlns:android="http://schemas.android.com/apk/res/android"
    xmlns:tools="http://schemas.android.com/tools"
    android:layout_width="match_parent"
    android:layout_height="match_parent">

    <TextView
        android:id="@+id/hello_world"
        android:text="@string/hello_world"
        android:layout_width="wrap_content"
        android:layout_height="wrap_content" />
```

```
<Button
    android:id="@+id/button"
    android:text="@string/button_label"
    android:layout_width="wrap_content"
    android:layout_height="wrap_content" />
```

```
</RelativeLayout>
```

You can apply the layout resource to an activity as shown in Listing 4-13.

Listing 4-13. Applying the Layout Resource to Current Activity

```
setContentView(R.layout.activity_my);
```

Menu Resources

The *Menu*[7] resources define the structure of application menus such as the options menu, context menu, or submenus. Listing 4-14 defines the menu resources in XML format.

Listing 4-14. src/res/menu/my.xml Menu Resource File

```
<menu xmlns:android=
    "http://schemas.android.com/apk/res/android"
    xmlns:tools="http://schemas.android.com/tools"
    tools:context=".MyActivity" >
    <item android:id="@+id/action_settings"
        android:title="@string/action_settings"
        android:orderInCategory="100"
        android:showAsAction="never" />
</menu>
```

Listing 4-15 demonstrates how to reference the menu resource through the R.menu.<resource file name>.

Listing 4-15. Using the Menu Resource in the Code

```
getMenuInflater().inflate(R.menu.my, menu);
```

---

[7]http://developer.android.com/guide/topics/resources/menu-resource.html.

Raw Resources

The raw resources are resources that do not belong to any of these resource groups. Android expects them to be in the src/res/raw directory. The raw resources do not have to be XML files like the other resource types; they can be in any format. You can reference them in the code as R.raw.<resource file name> without the file extension. As shown in Listing 4-16, you can use the Resources.openRawResource[8] method to open a data stream for reading the raw resource, src/res/raw/attributions.txt, in the code.

Listing 4-16. Using the Raw Resource in the Code

```
InputStream inputStream =
        getResources().openRawResource(R.raw.attributions);
```

Value Resources

The value resources are simple values, such as strings, integers, Booleans, and colors. Android expects the value resource files to be placed in the src/res/values directory. Values resource files are provided in XML format. A single value resource file can contain multiple value resources.

As each resource is identified with its own ID, Android gives the developer the flexibility to organize the value in whatever way makes sense. For example, you can place all color resources in colors.xml, or you can have individual resource files per activity for clarity. An example resource file looks as shown in Listing 4-17.

Listing 4-17. src/res/values/strings.xml Value Resources File

```
<?xml version="1.0" encoding="utf-8"?>
<resources>
    <string name="app_name">Hello Android</string>

    <bool name="registered">false</bool>

    <color name="title_background">#ffff0000</color>

    <dimen name="activity_horizontal_margin">16dp</dimen>

    <integer name="count">10</integer>
```

---

[8]http://developer.android.com/reference/android/content/res/Resources.html#openRawResource(int).

```
    <integer-array name="numbers">
        <item>1</item>
        <item>2</item>
    </integer-array>
</resources>
```

String Resources

String resources are simple text strings. We define a simple string resource through the <string>[9] XML tag, as shown in Listing 4-18.

Listing 4-18. Defining a String Resource

```
<string name="app_name">Hello Android</string>
```

You can then reference the string resource from the application code using the getString[10] method and referencing to it through R.string.<resource name>, as shown in Listing 4-19.

Listing 4-19. Using the String Resource in the Code

```
String appName = getString(R.string.app_name);
```

> **Note** For localization of string resources, please refer to the section "Default and Alternative Resources," in this chapter.

String Arrays

You can also define string arrays in the value resources using the <string-array>[11] XML tag, as shown in Listing 4-20.

Listing 4-20. Defining a String Array Resource in the Value Resources File

```
<string-array name="android_versions">
    <item>KitKat</item>
    <item>Lollipop</item>
</string-array>
```

---

[9]http://developer.android.com/guide/topics/resources/string-resource.html#String.
[10]http://developer.android.com/reference/android/content/Context.html#getString(int).
[11]http://developer.android.com/guide/topics/resources/string-resource.html#StringArray.

After defining the string array resource in the resource file, you can use it in the code through the getStringArray[12] method by providing its resource ID as R.array.<resource name>, as shown in Listing 4-21.

Listing 4-21. Using the String Array Resource in the Application Code

```
String[] androidVersions =
      getResources().getStringArray(R.array.android_versions);
```

Quantity Strings

Languages have different grammatical rules for plurals. Android provides a special resource type to define quantity strings in value resources. We define these resources using the <plurals> XML tag as shown in Listing 4-22.

Listing 4-22. Defining Plural Value Resources

```
<plurals name="books_found">
    <item quantity="zero">No books found.</item>
    <item quantity="one">One book found.</item>
    <item quantity="few">Few books found.</item>
    <item quantity="many">So many books found.</item>
    <item quantity="other">%d books found.</item>
</plurals>
```

The <plural> XML tag contains one or more <item> tags for plurals that require special treatment. The quantity attribute of the <item> tag indicates the plural case for which the string should be used. Table 4-2 provides a list of all plural cases that are supported.

Table 4-2. List of Plural Quantities That Can Have Special Treatment

Quantity	Description
zero	Special treatment for number 0.
one	Special treatment for number 1.
two	Special treatment for number 2.
few	Special treatment for small numbers.
many	Special treatment for large numbers.
other	For any other given number. (The %d can be used number substitution).

---

[12]http://developer.android.com/reference/android/content/res/Resources.html#getStringArray(int).

You can obtain the plural string resources through the `getQuantityString` method by providing their unique resource ID through the `R.plurals.<resource name>` as shown in Listing 4-23.

Listing 4-23. Using the Plural String Resources from the Application Code

```
String zeroBooksFound = getResources().getQuantityString(
        R.plurals.books_found, 0, 0);

String eightBooksFound = getResources().getQuantityString(
        R.plurals.books_found, 8, 8);
```

> **Note**   You need to pass the quantity twice if your plural strings include string formatting with a number, such as %d books found. The first parameter is used to select the proper string, and the second parameter is passed to the string formatter for %d substitution.

Boolean Resources

You can define Boolean value resources using the `<bool>`[13] XML tag as shown in Listing 4-24.

Listing 4-24. Defining a Boolean Value Resource

```
<bool name="registered">false</bool>
```

The Booleans can then be referenced from the application code using the `Resources.getBoolean`[14] method and by providing the unique resource ID through `R.bool.<resource name>` constant as shown in Listing 4-25.

Listing 4-25. Using the Boolean Value Resource from the Application Code

```
boolean registered = getResources().getBoolean(
        R.bool.registered);
```

---

[13]http://developer.android.com/guide/topics/resources/more-resources. html#Bool.

[14]http://developer.android.com/reference/android/content/res/ Resources.html#getBoolean(int).

Color Resources

You can define the color value resources using the `<color>`[15] XML tag as shown in Listing 4-26.

Listing 4-26. Defining a Color Value Resource

```
<color name="title_background">#ffff0000</color>
```

The color values are specified using the *RGB color model*[16] where the red, green, and blue (RGB) lights are added together to produce the color. In addition to the color components, you can also provide an Alpha value to specify the transparency. The RGB color components can be specified using any of the following formats as shown in Table 4-3 where the values are in hex.

Table 4-3. Formats That Can Be Used to Specify the Color Resource

Format	Description	Example
#RGB	Red-Green-Blue with single hex digit precision (0 to F).	#F00 (red)
#ARGB	Alpha-Red-Green-Blue with single hex digit precision (0 to F).	#60F0 (green with transparency)
#RRGGBB	Red-Green-Blue with double hex digit precision (0 to FF).	#FF0000 (red)
#AARRGGBB	Alpha-Red-Green-Blue with double hex digit precision (0 to FF).	#6200FF00 (green with transparency)

You can reference the color resources in the application code using the `Resources.getColor` method and by providing the unique resource ID through the `R.color.<resource name>` constant as shown in Listing 4-27.

Listing 4-27. Using the Color Resource in the Application Code

```
int backgroundColor = getResources().getColor(
      R.color.title_background);
```

---

[15]http://developer.android.com/guide/topics/resources/more-resources.html#Color.
[16]http://en.wikipedia.org/wiki/RGB_color_model.

Dimension Resources

You can also specify the dimensions of UI components as part of the value resources using the `<dimension>`[17] XML tag as shown in Listing 4-28.

Listing 4-28. Defining the Dimension Resource

```
<dimen name="activity_horizontal_margin">16dp</dimen>
```

We specify the dimension value with a quantity followed by a unit of measure such as pixels, inches, and so on. Android supports the following units of measurement when defining dimension resources:

- `dp`: Density independent pixels are relative to 160 dpi screens on which 1dp is roughly equal to 1px. Depending on the screen density of the device, these numbers get scaled accordingly.

- `sp`: Scale independent pixels are the same as density independent pixels, but they also get scaled based on the user's font size preference. I recommend using this measurement unit when specifying the dimensions of text components.

- `pt`: Points are 1/72 of an inch based on the screen size.

- `px`: Pixels corresponds to the actual pixels on the screen.

- `mm`: Millimeters based on the physical size of the screen.

- `in`: Inches based on the physical size of the screen.

You can use the dimension resources in the application code with the `Resources.getDimension`[18] method and by providing the unique resource ID through the `R.dimen.<resource name>` constants as shown in Listing 4-29.

Listing 4-29. Using the Dimension Resource in the Application Code

```
float activityHorizontalMargin = getResources().getDimension(
        R.dimen.activity_horizontal_margin);
```

---

[17]http://developer.android.com/guide/topics/resources/more-resources. html#Dimension.
[18]http://developer.android.com/reference/android/content/res/Resources. html#getDimension(int).

The returned value, `activityHorizontalMargin`, is the resource dimension value multiplied with the appropriate metric. If you prefer the value in pixels, you can use the `Resources.getDimensionPixelSize`[19] method instead.

Integer Resources

You can also define simple integer numbers in the value resources using the `<integer>`[20] XML tag as shown in Listing 4-30.

Listing 4-30. Defining an Integer Value Resource

```
<integer name="count">10</integer>
```

We reference the integer resources in the application code using the `Resources.getInteger`[21] method and providing their unique resource ID through the `R.integer.<resource name>` constant as shown in Listing 4-31.

Listing 4-31. Using the Integer Resource in the Application Code

```
int count = getResources().getInteger(R.integer.count);
```

Integer Arrays

Just like the string arrays, integer arrays are also supported as value resources. You can define integer arrays in the value resource file using the `<integer-array>`[22] XML element as shown in Listing 4-32.

Listing 4-32. Defining an Integer Array Resource

```
<integer-array name="numbers">
    <item>1</item>
    <item>2</item>
</integer-array>
```

---

[19]http://developer.android.com/reference/android/content/res/Resources. html#getDimensionPixelSize(int).
[20]http://developer.android.com/guide/topics/resources/more-resources. html#Integer.
[21]http://developer.android.com/reference/android/content/res/Resources. html#getInteger(int).
[22]http://developer.android.com/guide/topics/resources/more-resources. html#IntegerArray.

You can reference the integer array resource in the application code by using the Resources.getIntArray[23] method and by providing the unique resource ID using the R.array.<resource name> constant as shown in Listing 4-33.

Listing 4-33. Using the Integer Array Resource in the Application Code

```
int[] numbers = getResources().getIntArray(R.array.numbers);
```

Typed Array Resources

The array support in resources is not limited by the string and integer arrays only. You can also define arrays of other resources (e.g., an array of drawables) as a typed array resource using the <array>[24] XML tag, as shown in Listing 4-34.

Listing 4-34. Defining a Typed Array Resource

```
<array name="colors">
    <item>#FFF</item>
    <item>#000</item>
</array>
```

> **Note**   The typed arrays do not have to be homogeneous; Android also supports arrays of mixed resource types.

You can reference the types of array resources in the application code using the Resources.obtainTypedArray[25] method and by providing the unique resource ID through R.array.<resource name> constant. You can then obtain the elements of the array through the appropriate method of content.res.TypeArray[26] class for the underlying resource type, as shown in Listing 4-35.

---

[23]http://developer.android.com/reference/android/content/res/Resources.html#getIntArray(int).

[24]http://developer.android.com/guide/topics/resources/more-resources.html#TypedArray.

[25]http://developer.android.com/reference/android/content/res/Resources.html#obtainTypedArray(int).

[26]http://developer.android.com/reference/android/content/res/TypedArray.html.

Listing 4-35. Using the Typed Array Resource from the Application Code

```
TypedArray colors = getResources().obtainTypedArray(
        R.array.colors);

int background = colors.getColor(0, Color.BLACK);
int foreground = colors.getColor(1, Color.WHITE);
```

XML Resources

The XML resources are arbitrary XML formatted resource files. Compared to the raw resources, the Android toolchain does some pre-parsing of the XML resources at build time. This makes the XML resources much quicker to use during the runtime. Android expects them to be in the `src/res/xml` directory. You can access the XML resources by calling the `Resources.` `getXml`[27] method and providing a reference to the resource through the `R.xml.<resource file name>` as shown in Listing 4-36.

Listing 4-36. Reading the XML Resource Using the XML Pull Parser

```
XmlResourceParser xmlResourceParser =
        getResources().getXml(R.xml.configuration);

try {
    for (int eventType = xmlResourceParser.getEventType();
            eventType != XmlPullParser.END_DOCUMENT;
            eventType = xmlResourceParser.next()) {

        switch (eventType) {
            case XmlPullParser.START_TAG:
                String tagName = xmlResourceParser.getName();
                break;

            case XmlPullParser.TEXT:
                String text = xmlResourceParser.getText();
                break;

            case XmlPullParser.END_TAG:
                String tagName = xmlResourceParser.getName();
                break;
        }
    }
} catch (XmlPullParserException e) {
```

---

[27]http://developer.android.com/reference/android/content/res/Resources. html#getXml(int).

```
    e.printStackTrace();
} catch (IOException e) {
    e.printStackTrace();
}
```

The getXml method returns a content.res.XmlResourceParser[28] instance that can be used to parse the XML resource using an XML pull parser.

Default and Alternative Resources

Besides the default set of resources, Android applications can also contain alternative resources for different device configurations, such as alternative string resources to address different languages and alternative drawable resources to cover different screen densities. At runtime, Android picks the right set of resources based on the current device configuration.

Defining Alternative Resources

We place alternative resources in a separate resource directory which is named as <resource directory>-<configuration qualifier>, such as values-tr for value resources in the Turkish language.

> **Caution**   The alternative resource files should have the same name as the default resource files, as the names are used as the unique resource ID when referring to them in the application code.

Supported Configuration Qualifiers

You can also specify more than one configuration qualifier by simply adding them to the directory name separated by a dash, such as values-tr-car for value resources in the Turkish language when the device is displaying on a car dock. When you use multiple configuration qualifiers, they must be in the order in which they are listed in Table 4-4.

---

[28]http://developer.android.com/reference/android/content/res/XmlResource Parser.html.

Table 4-4. Supported Configuration Qualifier Names

Configuration	Description	Example
MCC/MNC	Mobile Country Code (MCC)[29] and Mobile Network Operator (MNC).	mcc310 mcc310-mnc004
Language and Region	Language is defined either by two-letter ISO 639-1[30] language code or by ISO 3166-1-alpha-2[31] region code.	en tr-rTR
Layout Direction	Left-to-right (default) or right-to-left (i.e., Arabic language).	ldltr (left to right) ldrtl (right to left)
Smallest Width	Shortest dimension of available screen size. This won't change based on device's orientation.	sw480dp (handset) sw600dp (tablet)
Available Width	Available screen width in dp unit. This can change when the device orientation changes.	w720dp
Available Height	Available screen height in dp unit. This can change when the device orientation changes.	h720dp
Screen Size	Screen size similar to a low-density QVGA screen with minimum size of 320x426 dp is represented as small.	small
	Screen size similar to a medium-density HVGA screen with minimum size of 320x470 dp is represented as medium.	normal
	Screen size similar to a medium-density VGA screen with minimum size of 480x640 dp is represented as large.	large
	Screen size similar to a medium-density HVGA with minimum size of 720x960 dp is represented as xlarge.	xlarge

(continued)

---

[29]http://en.wikipedia.org/wiki/Mobile_country_code.
[30]http://www.loc.gov/standards/iso639-2/php/code_list.php.
[31]http://www.iso.org/iso/en/prods-services/iso3166ma/02iso-3166-code-lists/list-en1.html.

Table 4-4. (*continued*)

Configuration	Description	Example
Screen Aspect	Based on the aspect ratio, a wide screen is represented as long, such as WQVGA, WVGA, and FWVGA. And as notlong such as QVGA, HVGA, and VGA.	long notlong
Screen Orientation	The orientation of the screen, port for portrait, and land for landscape. This can change when the device orientation changes.	port land
UI Mode	Device is in a car dock. Device is in a desk dock. Device is displaying on a television. Device is serving as an appliance. Device is worn as a watch.	car desk television watch
Night Mode	Night time is night, and day time is notnight.	night notnight
Screen Density	Low density is ldpi ~ 120 dpi	ldpi
	Medium density is mdpi ~ 160 dpi	mdpi
	High density is hdpi ~ 240 dpi	hdpi
	Extra high density is xhdpi ~ 320 dpi	xhdpi
	Extra-extra high density is xxhdpi ~ 480 dpi	xxhdpi
	Extra-extra-extra high density is xxxhdpi ~ 640 dpi	xxxhdpi
	The nodpi is used for resources that should not scale.	nodpi
	Televisions are tvdpi ~ 213 dpi	tvdpi
Touchscreen	Device with no touchscreen is represented as notouch; with touchscreen represented as finger.	notouch finger
Keyboard	Keyboard is exposed is represented as keysexposed.	keysexposed
	The device has a hidden hardware keyboard and the software keyboard is disabled represented as keyshidden.	keyshidden
	Device with software keyboard available is represented as keyssoft.	keyssoft

(*continued*)

Table 4-4. (*continued*)

Configuration	Description	Example
Primary Input	Device with no keys for input is represented as nokeys. Device with hardware qwerty keyboard is represented as qwerty. Device with a hardware 12-key keyboard is 12key.	nokeys qwerty 12key
Navigation Key	Navigation keys available is represented as navexposed; otherwise navhidden.	navexposed navhidden
Primary Non-Touch Navigation Method	Device with no navigation other than touchscreen is represented as nonav. Device with a directional pad is represented as dpad. Device with a trackball is represented as trackball. Device with directional wheel(s) is represented as wheel.	nonav dpad trackball wheel
Platform Version	The API level supported by the device.	v3 v4

Note To use a resource in more than one configuration, you can create an alias resource for the XML counterpart, such as *XML bitmap* for image resources.

Handling Runtime Changes

The Android framework restarts the activities when it detects a change in device configuration, such as a device orientation change or the user changing the device's language. When the Android framework restarts the activity, the proper resources based on the new device configuration load seamlessly.

If the application prefers to handle the configuration change without the activity being restarted, it should declare the list of configuration changes that are handled by the application in the application manifest, as shown in Listing 4-37.

Listing 4-37. Configuration Changes That Are Handled by the Application

```
<activity
    android:name=".MyActivity"
    android:label="@string/app_name"
    android:configChanges="orientation">
```

Once the Android framework detects the device configuration change, instead of restarting the activity, it simply calls the Activity.onConfigurationChanged[32] method of the activity. The application is expected to override this method to handle the device configuration change.

Assets

Another way of bundling artifacts with the applications is the assets. Android expects the assets to be present in the src/main/assets directory. Compared to the resources, the assets do not get processed by the Android toolchain and they maintain their original final names and their directory structure. There are no unique resource IDs for the artifacts in the assets directory, as they can be accessed through their original file names. The application can use the content of the assets directory through the methods of the content.res.AssetManager[33] class. You can obtain an instance of AssetManager through the getAssets[34] method of the current context, as shown in Listing 4-38.

Listing 4-38. Using the Artifacts in the Assets Directory in the Application Code

```
try {
    InputStream inputStream = getAssets().open("file.dat");
    try {

    } finally {
        inputStream.close();
    }
} catch (IOException e) {
    e.printStackTrace();
}
```

---

[32]http://developer.android.com/reference/android/app/Activity.html#on ConfigurationChanged(android.content.res.Configuration).
[33]http://developer.android.com/reference/android/content/res/Asset Manager.html.
[34]http://developer.android.com/reference/android/content/Context.html #getAssets().

Using Assets in Web View

Assets become very handy when bundling web pages with the application, such as HTML, CSS, JS, and image files. You can place these files into the assets directory keeping their original names and structure. The Android `android.webkit.WebView`[35] instance can then easily load them through a specific file URL (uniform resource locator), `file:///android_asset/<file name>`, as shown in Listing 4-39.

Listing 4-39. Web View Loading the Web Page from the Assets Directory

```
WebView webView = (WebView) findViewById(R.id.web_view);
webView.loadUrl("file:///android_assets/index.html");
```

APK Expansion Files

The Google Play application store currently requires the application packages not to exceed 50MB. Although this is lots of space for most applications, some applications, such as games, may require code and assets. In order to overcome this issue, Google Play allows attaching up to two *APK expansion files*,[36] each up to 2GB, to the application package. We refer to the first one as the `main` expansion file, and the latter as the `patch` expansion file. As indicated by its name, the second one is assumed to be updating the main expansion file.

> **Note**   Although the second expansion file is for patching the main expansion file, if 2GB is not enough to bundle all required resources for the application, you can use the second expansion file as the additional resource file, which will make it possible to have 4GB of extra resources accompanying the application package.

---

[35]http://developer.android.com/reference/android/webkit/WebView.html.
[36]http://developer.android.com/google/play/expansion-files.html.

These expansion files automatically download when you install the application on the device, and they are placed into the external storage under the `<external storage>/Android/obb/<application package>` directory. Google Play does not require any specific format for the expansion files.

Summary

In this section I described how to attach various resources to your Android application. Through the list of configuration qualifiers provided in this chapter, you can obtain an alternative set of resources within the same application to cover more device configurations. Android provides a comprehensive resource management framework that can automatically find the best resource for a device configuration and also update it in real time when it detects a device configuration change. In the next chapters, you will learn how to use the attached resources with the UI components.

Chapter 5

Layouts and Views

The Android platform provides a comprehensive UI framework for mobile applications to provide easy-to-use and consistent user interfaces. This chapter covers the supported static and dynamic layouts, user interface components for both input and output, and the Fragment API (application programming interface) to develop modular and reusable user interface parts.

Layouts

On the Android platform, the visual structure of the application's user interface is defined through the layouts. Each layout type is a subclass of the ViewGroup class. The layout can contain individual View and also other ViewGroup elements. As a ViewGroup flavor, the layout is responsible for providing the necessary logic to position and draw its elements on the screen.

Declaring Layouts

The Android framework supports two approaches to declare the layout and its elements.

 - **Using the XML resources:** The layout and its elements can be defined in XML-formatted resource files using a straightforward XML vocabulary. This enables the application to separate the presentation and the business logic. As Android supports different screen sizes and densities, the application can simply provide different XML layout resources per each target display size.

> **Tip** The Android Studio IDE (integrated development environment) provides the necessary tools to visually manipulate the layout files during development.

- **Programmatically using the API:** The Android framework provides the necessary user interface classes and methods to declare and manipulate the layout and its elements programmatically from within the application.

In order to make it easier to use, the XML vocabulary for declaring the layout and its elements closely follows the naming and structure of the actual API.

Although there are two supported approaches, we recommend that you use the XML layout resource files to define the Android user interfaces, unless they are not applicable due to the unique requirements of the application.

Layout Requirements

For layouts to function properly, they need to know the size of all of their child elements, including the nested View and ViewGroup elements. For that reason, the following two attributes are required to be set by all View and ViewGroup elements:

- `android:layout_width`: The width of the element.
- `android:layout_height`: The height of the element.

Both of those width and height attributes can either take a numeric size value or simply a constant based on the expected size behavior. The supported constant values are:

- `matchParent`: View wants to be as big as its parent.
- `wrapContent`: View wants to be just big enough to enclose its content.

Common Layouts

The Android framework provides a set of common layouts to address most frequent use cases. Through these common layouts, you can define all kinds of static user interfaces.

Linear Layout

The LinearLayout[1] organizes its elements in a linear fashion either as a horizontal or a vertical row, as shown in Figure 5-1.

Figure 5-1. LinearLayout with elements organized in horizontal and vertical rows

Linear Layout Orientation

The android:orientation[2] attribute of the LinearLayout XML element specifies the orientation of the LinearLayout, as shown in Listing 5-1.

Listing 5-1. LinearLayout with Orientation Set to Vertical

```
<LinearLayout
    xmlns:android="http://schemas.android.com/apk/res/android"
    android:layout_width="match_parent"
    android:layout_height="match_parent"
    android:orientation="vertical">

    ...

</LinearLayout>
```

---

[1]http://developer.android.com/reference/android/widget/LinearLayout.html.
[2]http://developer.android.com/reference/android/widget/LinearLayout
.html#attr_android:orientation.

The android:orientation attribute can take the following values:

- horizontal: Organized as a horizontal row.
- vertical: Organized as a vertical row.

If the android:orientation attribute is not provided, the default orientation for the LinearLayout is horizontal.

Linear Layout Weight

The LinearLayout, based on the available screen real estate and its orientation, adjusts the size of its child elements to fill the available space. This enables the user interface to adapt to various screen sizes automatically.

By default, the space distribution is done equally for each child element; however, as shown in Listing 5-2, through the android:layout_weight[3] attribute different weights can be assigned to each child element.

Listing 5-2. LinearLayout with the First Element Taking a Larger Weight

```
<LinearLayout
    xmlns:android="http://schemas.android.com/apk/res/android"
    android:layout_width="match_parent"
    android:layout_height="match_parent"
    android:orientation="horizontal">

    <Button
        android:id="@+id/button_1"
        android:layout_width="wrap_content"
        android:layout_height="wrap_content"
        android:layout_weight="1"
        android:text="@string/button_1"/>

    <Button
        android:id="@+id/button_2"
        android:layout_width="wrap_content"
        android:layout_height="wrap_content"
        android:text="@string/button_2"/>

</LinearLayout>
```

---

[3]http://developer.android.com/reference/android/widget/LinearLayout.LayoutParams.html#attr_android:layout_weight.

As shown in Figure 5-2, a larger weight allows the child element to expand and fill a larger space on the screen than other child elements with a lower weight.

Figure 5-2. LinearLayout with a first child element taking a larger screen space

If the android:layout_weight attribute is not specified, the default weight is zero.

Linear Layout Gravity

By default, the LinearLayout positions its elements aligned with the top edge. The android:layout_gravity[4] attribute can be used to change this default behavior. The android:layout_gravity attribute can take one or more values to specify how the View element should be positioned on the screen.

Supported Values in Horizontal Orientation

The following values are supported in horizontal orientation mode:

> top: Position the View at the top of its container.

> center_vertical: Position the View in the vertical center of its container.

> bottom: Position the View to the bottom of its container.

Supported Values in Vertical Orientation

The following values are supported in vertical orientation mode:

> left: Position the View to the left of its container.

> center_horizontal: Position the View in the horizontal center of its container.

> right: Position the View to the right of its container.

---

[4]http://developer.android.com/reference/android/widget/LinearLayout.
LayoutParams.html#attr_android:layout_gravity.

Relative Layout

Almost all kinds of user interfaces can be designed by simply nesting multiple LinearLayouts; however, this will also result in a very complex layout file that is hard to maintain and manipulate. The Android framework provides the RelativeLayout[5] to design complex user interfaces, as shown in Figure 5-3, without any nesting of layouts.

Figure 5-3. RelativeLayout with child elements positioned relative to each other

The RelativeLayout organizes its elements relative to each other. The position of each child element can be specified as relative to its siblings or its parent. Each child element of a RelativeLayout takes one or more layout-specific attributes to provide hints about how they should be positioned on the screen, as shown in Listing 5-3.

Listing 5-3. RelativeLayout with Child Elements Providing Hints for Their Position

```
<RelativeLayout
    xmlns:android="http://schemas.android.com/apk/res/android"
    android:layout_width="match_parent"
    android:layout_height="match_parent"
    android:padding="20dp">

    <EditText
        android:id="@+id/edit_username"
        android:layout_width="wrap_content"
        android:layout_height="wrap_content"
        android:layout_alignParentTop="true"
        android:layout_alignParentEnd="true"
        android:layout_toEndOf="@+id/label_username" />
```

---

[5]http://developer.android.com/reference/android/widget/RelativeLayout.html.

```
<TextView
    android:id="@+id/label_username"
    android:layout_width="wrap_content"
    android:layout_height="wrap_content"
    android:layout_alignBaseline="@id/edit_username"
    android:text="Username:" />

<Button
    android:id="@+id/button_login"
    android:layout_width="wrap_content"
    android:layout_height="wrap_content"
    android:layout_below="@id/edit_username"
    android:layout_alignLeft="@id/edit_username"
    android:text="Login" />

<CheckBox
    android:id="@+id/checkbox_remember_username"
    android:layout_width="wrap_content"
    android:layout_height="wrap_content"
    android:layout_below="@id/edit_username"
    android:layout_alignParentRight="true"
    android:layout_alignBottom="@id/button_login"
    android:text="Remember username?" />
```

k</RelativeLayout>

Positioning Relative to an Anchor View

The following RelativeLayout attributes position the View relative to a
specified anchor View:[6]

- android:layout_above: Position the bottom edge above
  the specified anchor.

- android:layout_alignBaseline: Position the baseline
  on the baseline of the specified anchor view.

- android:layout_alignBottom: Position the bottom edge
  to match that of the specified anchor view.

- android:layout_alignEnd: Position the end edge to
  match that of the specified anchor view.

- android:layout_alignLeft: Position the left edge to
  match that of the specified anchor view.

- android:layout_alignRight: Position the right edge to
  match that of the specified anchor view.

---

[6]http://developer.android.com/reference/android/widget/RelativeLayout
.LayoutParams.html

- `android:layout_alignStart`: Position the start edge to match that of the specified anchor view.

- `android:layout_alignTop`: Position the top edge to match that of the specified anchor view.

- `android:layout_below`: Position the top edge below that of the specified anchor view.

- `android:layout_toEndOf`: Position the start edge to match the end edge of the specified anchor view.

- `android:layout_toLeftOf`: Position the right edge to match the left edge of the specified anchor view.

- `android:layout_toRightOf`: Position the left edge to match the right edge of the specified anchor view.

- `android:layout_toStartOf`: Position the end edge to match the start edge of the specified anchor view.

Positioning Relative to Parent View

The following `RelativeLayout` attributes position the `View` relative to its parent `View`:

- `android:layout_alignParentBottom`: Position the bottom edge to match that of the parent view.

- `android:layout_alignParentEnd`: Position the end edge to match that of the parent view.

- `android:layout_alignParentLeft`: Position the left edge to match that of the parent view.

- `android:layout_alignParentRight`: Position the right edge to match that of the parent view.

- `android:layout_alignParentStart`: Position the start edge to match that of the parent view.

- `android:layout_alignParentTop`: Position the top edge to match that of the parent view.

- `android:layout_centerHorizontal`: If true, centers this view horizontally within its parent.

- `android:layout_centerInParent`: If true, centers this view both horizontally and vertically within its parent.

- `android:layout_centerVertical`: If true, centers this view vertically within its parent.

> **Tip** In case the anchor view is not visible, the android:layout_ alignWithParentIfMissing attribute can be set to true so that the parent will be used as the anchor when the specified anchor view cannot be found.

Dynamic Layouts

The common layouts that are provided by the Android framework are more suitable for static user interfaces, where the elements of the user interface are predetermined. When the content of a user interface is not predetermined, the Android framework provides the AdapterView[7] layout to support the development of dynamic user interfaces. The AdapterView layout populates the user interface at runtime by relying on a provided Adapter[8] instance as its gateway to dynamic content.

Adapter

The Adapter behaves as a bridge between the data source and the AdapterView layout. It retrieves the data and converts each entity into a View that can be added into the AdapterView layout. The Android framework provides several subclasses of Adapter to facilitate the retrieval of data from most common data sources, such as arrays and databases.

Array Adapter

The ArrayAdapter[9] is a subclass of the Adapter class. As shown in Listing 5-4, it takes the current context, an array instance holding the data, and a layout resource to create View instances for each data element.

Listing 5-4. ArrayAdapter Instance Based on a Given String Array

```
ArrayAdapter<String> arrayAdapter = new ArrayAdapter<String>(
        this,
        android.R.layout.simple_list_item_1,
        new String[] {
                "Item 1",
                "Item 2",
```

---

[7]http://developer.android.com/reference/android/widget/AdapterView.html.
[8]http://developer.android.com/reference/android/widget/Adapter.html.
[9]http://developer.android.com/reference/android/widget/ArrayAdapter.html.

```
                "Item 3",
                "Item 4"
        }
);
```

> **Note** The android.R.layout.simple_list_item_1 refers to the
> simple list item layout resource that the Android framework itself provides.
> Other layout resources that the Android framework provides can be found
> in the android.R.layout[10] class.

The provided layout resource must contain a TextView that will be populated
by the ArrayAdapter, as shown in Listing 5-5. The toString method of
each array element will be called to translate the object into text in order to
populate the TextView.

Listing 5-5. Layout Resource Formed by a Single TextView to Display Each Item

```
<TextView
    xmlns:android="http://schemas.android.com/apk/res/android"
    android:id="@android:id/text1"
    android:layout_width="fill_parent"
    android:layout_height="wrap_content"
    android:gravity="center_vertical"
    android:paddingLeft="6dip" />
```

> **Note** The ArrayAdapter assumes that the given layout resource for a
> single data item is only a TextView. If the layout resource is a composite
> of multiple other View elements, then the View ID of the TextView can
> be supplied to ArrayAdapter through its constructor.[11]

---

[10]http://developer.android.com/reference/android/R.layout.html.
[11]http://developer.android.com/reference/android/widget/ArrayAdapter
.html #ArrayAdapter(android.content.Context, int, int, T[]).

Simple Cursor Adapter

The ArrayAdapter assumes that the data is entirely loaded into memory at the time the Adapter instance is initiated. In most cases, the data exists on a database, and loading the entire data set into memory is not a preferred approach. The Android framework provides the SimpleCursorAdapter[12] to allow applications to populate AdapterView layouts with data coming from a database.

As shown in Listing 5-6, the SimpleCursorAdapter takes a layout resource for the data items, a Cursor instance to pull the data from, and two arrays to map between the data columns and the corresponding View elements in the given layout resource.

Listing 5-6. SimpleCursorAdapter Retrieving Data from a Given Cursor Instance

```
SimpleCursorAdapter cursorAdapter = new SimpleCursorAdapter(
        this,
        R.layout.list_item,
        cursor,
        new String[] {
                "name",
                "email"
        },
        new int[] {
                R.id.name,
                R.id.email
        }
);
```

> **Note**   Chapter 7 discusses the Cursor class and usage of databases in Android applications.

Custom Adapter

The ArrayAdapter and the SimpleCursorAdapter are not the only Adapter types available. If neither one of them is suitable for the unique requirements of the application, a custom Adapter can be subclassed from the BaseAdapter.[13] As the BaseAdapter is an abstract class, the subclass is expected to provide implementations of certain Adapter methods.

---

[12]http://developer.android.com/reference/android/widget/SimpleCursor Adapter.html.
[13]http://developer.android.com/reference/android/widget/BaseAdapter.html.

The getCount Method

The getCount[14] method is expected to return the number of items in the data set, as shown in Listing 5-7.

Listing 5-7. Overriding the getCount Method of the Adapter Class

```
@Override
public int getCount() {
    // Return the number of items in the data set
    return 4;
}
```

The getItem Method

The getItem[15] method is expected to return the item object at the given position, as shown in Listing 5-8.

Listing 5-8. Overriding the getItem Method of the Adapter Class

```
@Override
public Object getItem(int position) {
    // Return the object at given position
    return "Item " + position;
}
```

The getItemId Method

The getItemId[16] method is expected to return the row ID for a given position. If there is no separate ID to return, the application can simply return the given position as the ID, as shown in Listing 5-9.

Listing 5-9. Overriding the getItemId Method of the Adapter Class

```
@Override
public long getItemId(int position) {
    // Return the ID of the object at given position
    return position;
}
```

---

[14] http://developer.android.com/reference/android/widget/Adapter.html#getCount().
[15] http://developer.android.com/reference/android/widget/Adapter.html#getItem(int).
[16] http://developer.android.com/reference/android/widget/Adapter.html#getItemId(int).

The getView Method

The getView[17] method is expected to return a fully populated View object that can be added to the AdapterView layout to display the data item. The application can either create a new View programmatically or simply inflate a layout resource. The getView method, as its second parameter, receives an old View instance to reuse, if possible, as shown in Listing 5-10.

Listing 5-10. Overriding the getView Method of the Adapter Class

```
@Override
public View getView(int position,
                    View convertView,
                    ViewGroup parent) {
    // Return a fully populated View instance

    TextView textView;

    if (convertView == null) {
        // Inflate the view resource
        LayoutInflater layoutInflater =
                (LayoutInflater) context.getSystemService(
                    Context.LAYOUT_INFLATER_SERVICE);

        textView = (TextView) layoutInflater.inflate(
                android.R.layout.simple_list_item_1,
                parent, false);
    } else {
        // Reuse the existing view
        textView = (TextView) convertView;
    }

    Object item = getItem(position);

    textView.setText(item.toString());

    return textView;
}
```

The application should check the type of old View to make sure that it is not null and also that it is in appropriate type to display the data item. As its last parameter, the getView method takes the parent View instance that the View will eventually be attached to.

---

[17]http://developer.android.com/reference/android/widget/Adapter.html#
getView(int, android.view.View, android.view.ViewGroup).

Notifying the Data Set Changes

After the AdapterView is populated, the data set may change at any given time. The AdapterView will not get refreshed automatically as it has no knowledge of the actual data source. The application is expected to call the notifyDataSetChanged[18] method to inform data set observers, including the AdapterView, as shown in Listing 5-11.

Listing 5-11.   Notify That the Data Set Has Changed and Needs to Be Refreshed

```
cursorAdapter.notifyDataSetChanged();
```

The ArrayAdapter provides helper methods to manipulate the data set, such as add and remove methods. If the application enabled the automatic data set to change notifications through the setNotifyOnChange[19] method, as shown in Listing 5-12, the ArrayAdapter will notify observers when the data set gets modified through these methods.

Listing 5-12. Enable Automatic Change Notifications for ArrayAdapter Methods

```
arrayAdapter.setNotifyOnChange(true);

arrayAdapter.add("Item 5");
arrayAdapter.remove("Item 4");
```

Adapter View Layout

The Android framework provide various flavors of the AdapterView layout for different use cases. All of these AdapterView subclasses take an Adapter instance to retrieve the actual data in the form of View instances to populate the content of the AdapterView on the screen. This section briefly touches on the most commonly used ones.

List View

The ListView[20] is an AdapterView layout that displays a list of scrollable items, as shown in Figure 5-4.

---

[18]http://developer.android.com/reference/android/widget/BaseAdapter.html #notifyDataSetChanged().
[19]http://developer.android.com/reference/android/widget/ArrayAdapter. html #setNotifyOnChange(boolean).
[20]http://developer.android.com/reference/android/widget/ListView.html.

Figure 5-4. *ListView displaying four items*

It can be declared in a layout resource file using the ListView XML tag, as shown in Listing 5-13.

Listing 5-13. Adding the ListView to a Layout Resource

```
<ListView
    android:id="@+id/list"
    android:layout_width="match_parent"
    android:layout_height="match_parent" />
```

The ListView takes the ListAdapter[21] instance through its setAdapter[22] method, as shown in Listing 5-14.

Listing 5-14. Providing the ListAdapter to the ListView

```
ListView listView = (ListView) findViewById(R.id.list);
listView.setAdapter(arrayAdapter);
```

---

[21]http://developer.android.com/reference/android/widget/ListAdapter.html.
[22]http://developer.android.com/reference/android/widget/ListView.html#
setAdapter(android.widget.ListAdapter).

The ListAdapter is simply a subclass of the Adapter class, and it simply introduces two additional methods to it. Those methods are areAllItemsEnabled[23] and isEnabled. These methods become very useful when displaying certain rows as headers on the ListView. The Adapter's isEnabled[24] method can simply return false for these header rows to make them non-selectable.

Grid View

The GridView[25] is an AdapterView layout that displays items in a two-dimensional, scrollable grid, as shown in Figure 5-5.

Figure 5-5. GridView displaying the items as four columns

It can be declared in a layout resource file using the GridView XML tag, as shown in Listing 5-15.

Listing 5-15. Adding the GridView to a Layout Resource

```
<GridView
    android:id="@+id/grid"
    android:layout_width="match_parent"
    android:layout_height="match_parent"
    android:stretchMode="columnWidth"
    android:numColumns="4" />
```

---

[23]http://developer.android.com/reference/android/widget/ListAdapter .html#are AllItemsEnabled().
[24]http://developer.android.com/reference/android/widget/ListAdapter .html# isEnabled(int).
[25]http://developer.android.com/reference/android/widget/GridView.html.

The GridView XML tag also provides a set of attributes to allow the application to define characteristics of the GridView. The most notable of these attributes are

- android:columnWidth: Width of each column.

- android:gravity: Gravity of cell content.

- android:horizontalSpacing: Horizontal spacing between columns.

- android:numColumns: Number of columns to show.

- android:stretchMode: How columns should stretch to fill the empty space. It can take the following:

  - none: Stretching is disabled.

  - spacingWidth: Spacing between each column is stretched.

  - columnWidth: Each column is stretched.

  - spacingWidthUniform: Spacing between each column is uniformly stretched.

- android:verticalSpacing: Vertical spacing between rows.

All of these attributes can also be manipulated through the methods of the GridView class. Similar to the ListView, the GridView also takes a ListAdapter to populate its content through its setAdapter[26] method.

Spinner

The Spinner[27] is a subclass of the AdapterView layout. As shown in Figure 5-6, the Spinner provides an easy and quick way to present a dialog or a drop-down menu to allow the user to choose a single item from given list of items.

[26]http://developer.android.com/reference/android/widget/GridView.html#setAdapter(android.widget.ListAdapter).
[27]https://developer.android.com/reference/android/widget/Spinner.html.

Figure 5-6. *Spinner displaying the items as an inline drop-down menu*

It can be added to a layout resource using the `Spinner` XML tag, as shown in Listing 5-16.

Listing 5-16. *Adding the Spinner to a Layout Resource*

```
<Spinner
    android:id="@+id/spinner"
    android:layout_width="wrap_content"
    android:layout_height="wrap_content" />
```

The `Spinner` XML tag also provides a set of attributes to manipulate the characteristics of the `Spinner` instance. The most notable attributes are

- `android:spinnerMode`: Display mode for the `Spinner`. The supported modes are

  - `dialog`: The `Spinner` will be shown as a dialog window.

  - `dropdown`: The `Spinner` will be shown as an inline drop-down anchored to the spinner widget.

- `android:dropDownHorizontalOffset`: Number of pixels by which the drop-down should offset horizontally.

- `android:dropDownVerticalOffset`: Number of pixels by which the drop-down should offset vertically.

- `android:gravity`: Gravity for the content.

Supported Attributes in Drop-Down Spinner Mode

- `android:dropDownSelector`: Selector may be a reference to a resource or a color value.

■ android:dropDownWidth: Width of the drop-down.

■ android:popupBackground: Background drawable to use for the drop-down.

Supported Attributes in Dialog Spinner Mode

■ android:prompt: Prompt to display when the spinner dialog is shown.

Similar to the other AdapterView subclasses, the Spinner takes a SpinnerAdapter[28] to populate its content through its setAdapter[29] method.

Handling the Item Selection Events

The click events on an AdapterView get delivered to the application through the OnItemSelectedListener[30] interface. The application can register an OnItemSelectedListener instance with the AdapterView through the setOnItemSelectedListener[31] method, as shown in Listing 5-17.

Listing 5-17. Registering an OnItemSelectedListener Instance

```
spinner.setOnItemSelectedListener(
        new AdapterView.OnItemSelectedListener() {
    @Override
    public void onItemSelected(AdapterView<?> parent,
                                View view,
                                int position,
                                long id) {
        // Item selected
    }

    @Override
    public void onNothingSelected(AdapterView<?> parent) {
        // Nothing selected
    }
});
```

---

[28]http://developer.android.com/reference/android/widget/SpinnerAdapter.html.
[29]http://developer.android.com/reference/android/widget/Spinner.html#set Adapter(android.widget.SpinnerAdapter).
[30]http://developer.android.com/reference/android/widget/AdapterView .OnItem SelectedListener.html.
[31]http://developer.android.com/reference/android/widget/AdapterView .html# setOnItemSelectedListener(android.widget.AdapterView .OnItemSelected Listener).

The onItemSelected[32] method gets called when an item has been selected. The onNothingSelected[33] method gets called when the selection disappears.

Loading the XML Layout Resource

The XML-formatted layout resource files are placed in the src/res/layout subdirectory. The layout resource gets assigned a unique resource ID. Similar to other resources, a constant with the same name as the layout file gets generated in the R.layout class for this resource ID.

The setContentView method of the Activity class takes the layout resource ID to display the user interface, as shown in Listing 5-18.

Listing 5-18. Displaying the User Interface Using the Layout Resource

```
public class MainActivity extends Activity {
    @Override
    protected void onCreate(Bundle savedInstanceState) {
        super.onCreate(savedInstanceState);
        setContentView(R.layout.activity_main);
    }
}
```

Accessing Individual Views in a Layout

Once the corresponding user interface elements get created based on the given XML layout resource file, these elements can be individually accessed from the application code using their unique ID.

Assigning a Unique ID to a View Element

Besides the attributes that are specific to the type of the View itself, a set of common attributes are applicable to all types of View objects. The most frequently used one of these is the ID attribute. The ID attribute assigns a unique identifier to the View instance to make it possible for the application to refer to it at any given time. As shown in Listing 5-19, the XML attribute android:id is used to assign an ID to a View within a XML layout resource file.

---

[32]http://developer.android.com/reference/android/widget/AdapterView. OnItem SelectedListener.html#onItemSelected(android.widget. AdapterView<?>, android.view.View, int, long).
[33]http://developer.android.com/reference/android/widget/AdapterView. OnItem SelectedListener.html#onNothingSelected(android.widget. AdapterView<?>).

Listing 5-19. Assigning a Unique ID to a View

```
<Button
    android:id="@+id/button"
    android:layout_width="wrap_content"
    android:layout_height="wrap_content"
    android:text="@string/button_1"/>
```

Although a name is used as the unique ID in Listing 5-19, a resource ID in Android is an integer value. During compile time, the Android toolchain generates integer values for the ID names, as well as the R class in the application package with a list of constants that are mapping the ID names to the corresponding resource ID integer values. The + symbol in @+id/ button indicates that a new resource ID value should be generated by the Android toolchain, and it should be mapped to the name button.

Finding a View by Its Unique ID

As shown in Listing 5-20, the application can then refer to this user interface element by using the findViewById method of the Activity class and providing the View's unique ID through the constants provided in the R class.

Listing 5-20. Finding a View by Its Unique ID

```
Button button = (Button) findViewById(R.id.button);
```

Views

The View class represents the basic building block for all user interface components. A View instance occupies a rectangular area on the display, and it is responsible for drawing itself and handling events. The View components are used for both displaying information to the user and getting user input. In this section, we refer to these two View types as *output controls* and *input controls*, respectively.

Output Controls

The output controls are View subclasses used to present information to the user. Depending on the type of the View object, the displayed information can either be static, such as a text, or interactive, such as a progress bar.

TextView

The TextView[34] class allows displaying text to the user, as shown in Figure 5-7.

Figure 5-7. The TextView displaying a text with an e-mail as a link

A TextView can be added to the layout resource using the TextView XML tag, as shown in Listing 5-21.

Listing 5-21. Adding the TextView to a Layout Resource

```
<TextView
    android:layout_width="match_parent"
    android:layout_height="wrap_content"
    android:autoLink="all"
    android:ellipsize="end"
    android:singleLine="true"
    android:textSize="14sp"
    android:textStyle="normal"
    android:typeface="sans"
    android:textColor="#ff0000"
    android:text="Lorem ipsum dolor info@apress.com amet,
    consectetur adipiscing elit." />
```

Through the attributes of the XML tag, you can tune the features of the TextView instance. The TextView supports a long list of attributes.[35] The most notable ones are

---

[34]http://developer.android.com/reference/android/widget/TextView.html.
[35]http://developer.android.com/reference/android/R.styleable.
html#TextView.

- android:autoLink: If set, automatically converts links such as URLs (uniform resource locators) and e-mail addresses in the text to clickable links.

- android:ellipsize: If set, words that are longer than the available width get ellipsized instead of broken in the middle—such as start, middle, end.

- android:gravity: Text gravity, such as right|bottom.

- android:singleLine: If set, the text won't span to multiple lines.

- android:text: Text to display.

- android:textColor: Text color, such as #ff0000.

- android:textSize: Size of the text, such as 12sp.

- android:textStyle: Text style, such as bold, italic.

- android:typeface: Text typeface, such as normal, sans.

ImageView

The ImageView[36] class allows displaying an image to the user, such as an icon. The ImageView handles the scaling and tinting of the image in order to display it properly on the screen, as shown in Figure 5-8.

Figure 5-8. ImageView displaying the Apress logo

---

[36]http://developer.android.com/reference/android/widget/ImageView.html.

An ImageView can be added to the layout resource using the ImageView XML tag, as shown in Listing 5-22.

Listing 5-22. Adding the ImageView to a Layout Resource

```
<ImageView
    android:layout_width="wrap_content"
    android:layout_height="wrap_content"
    android:adjustViewBounds="true"
    android:cropToPadding="true"
    android:scaleType="matrix"
    android:src="@drawable/apress" />
```

The ImageView can also be customized through the XML attributes. The most notable attributes are

- android:adjustViewBounds: If set, adjusts its bounds to preserve the aspect ratio.

- android:cropToPadding: If set, crops the image to fit within its padding.

- android:scaleType: Controls how the image should be scaled, such as matrix, fitXY, fitStart, fitCenter, fitEnd, etc.

- android:src: Image source as a resource ID or a color.

- android:tint: Tinting color for the image.

- android:tintMode: Blending mode to apply image tint, such as multiply, add.

ProgressBar

The ProgressBar[37] allows the application to inform the user about the progress of an operation using a visual indicator. The ProgressBar displays a bar to indicate how far the operation has progressed, as shown in Figure 5-9. When the length of an operation is not known, the ProgressBar can be made indeterministic in order to simply show a cyclic animation, indicating a running operation.

---

[37]http://developer.android.com/reference/android/widget/ProgressBar.html.

Figure 5-9. ProgressBar in both horizontal and indeterminate modes

A ProgressBar can be added to a layout resource using the ProgressBar XML tag, as shown in Listing 5-23.

Listing 5-23. Adding the ProgressBar to a Layout Resource

```
<ProgressBar
    android:id="@+id/progress"
    android:layout_width="match_parent"
    android:layout_height="wrap_content"
    style="@android:style/Widget.ProgressBar.Horizontal"
    android:max="100"
    android:progress="20" />
```

Various features of the ProgressBar can be configured through the XML attributes[38] of the ProgressBar XML tag. The most notable ones are

- android:indeterminate: If set, enables the indeterminate mode.

- android:max: Maximum value the progress can take.

- android:progress: Progress value.

- style: The style for the ProgressBar; some of the styles that are provided by the Android platform are

    - @android:style/Widget.ProgressBar.Horizontal: Horizontal progress bar.

    - @android:style/Widget.ProgressBar.Small: Small spinner icon for indeterminate progress bar.

---

[38]http://developer.android.com/reference/android/R.styleable.html#ProgressBar.

- ▨ `@android:style/Widget.ProgressBar.Large`: Large spinner icon for indeterminate progress bar.

- ▨ `@android:style/Widget.ProgressBar.Inverse`: Reverse spinning icon for indeterminate progress bar.

Updating the Progress

During the runtime, the application can change the progress at any time, using the `setProgress`[39] method, as shown in Listing 5-24.

Listing 5-24. Updating the Progress Value of the ProgressBar Object

```
progressBar.setProgress(40);
```

> **Tip**   In order to provide a responsive user interface, Android applications should not occupy the UI thread for a long period of time. The `AsyncTask`[40] class can be used to process long-lasting operations on a separate thread, meanwhile updating the user interface asynchronously by overriding its `onProgressUpdate` and `onPostExecute` methods.

If the progress simply increments by a certain number, the `ProgressBar` also provides the `incrementProgressBy`[41] method to enable the application to simply increment the progress by a given value.

Space

The `Space`[42] is a lightweight `View` object that can be used to insert gaps between other components in both directions. A `Space` can be added to a layout resource using the `Space` XML tag. The `Space` XML tag does not take any additional attributes other than the mandatory `View` attributes, `android:layout_width` and `android:layout_height`. As shown in Listing 5-25, simply using these two attributes, any amount of gap can be inserted between other components.

---

[39]http://developer.android.com/reference/android/widget/ProgressBar.html #setProgress(int).
[40]http://developer.android.com/reference/android/os/AsyncTask.html.
[41]http://developer.android.com/reference/android/widget/ProgressBar.html #incrementProgressBy(int).
[42]http://developer.android.com/reference/android/widget/Space.html.

Listing 5-25. Adding the Space into a Layout Resource

```
<Space
    android:layout_width="wrap_content"
    android:layout_height="20dp" />
```

Input Controls

Input controls are interactive View components that can enable the user to interact with the application by providing input, such as a button. The Android platform provides a variety of input controls that can be used in applications.

EditText

The EditText[43] input control is a subclass of the TextView class. In addition to the features of a TextView, the EditText also enables the user to edit the content. An EditText can be added to a layout resource using the EditText XML tag, as shown in Listing 5-26.

Listing 5-26. Adding the EditText into a Layout Resource

```
<EditText
    android:id="@+id/edit"
    android:layout_width="match_parent"
    android:layout_height="wrap_content"
    android:autoText="true" />
```

The EditText XML tag also takes a set of attributes that can modify certain characteristics of the EditText instance; the most notable ones are

- android:autoText: If set, automatically corrects some of the common spelling errors.
- android:capitalize: If set, automatically capitalizes what the user types.
- android:cursorVisible: If set, makes the cursor visible.
- android:digit: If set, only accepts the numeric input.
- android:enabled: Specifies whether the control is enabled.

[43]http://developer.android.com/reference/android/widget/EditText.html.

■ android:password: If set, displays the characters as password dots instead of themselves.

■ android:phoneNumber: If set, enables the phone number input method.

Getting the Content of an EditText

The content of the EditText control can be retrieved through the getText[44] method, as shown in Listing 5-27.

Listing 5-27. Getting the Content of an EditText

```
String text = editText.getText().toString();
```

The getText method returns an Editable[45] object. It provides methods to append[46] to, replace,[47] and delete[48] ranges from the content of the EditText.

Button

The Button control provides a push button that can be clicked by the user, as shown in Figure 5-10.

Figure 5-10. The play button with a text and a play icon

---

[44]http://developer.android.com/reference/android/widget/EditText.html# getText().
[45]http://developer.android.com/reference/android/text/Editable.html.
[46]http://developer.android.com/reference/android/text/Editable. html#append (java.lang.CharSequence).
[47]http://developer.android.com/reference/android/text/Editable. html#replace (int, int, java.lang.CharSequence, int, int).
[48]http://developer.android.com/reference/android/text/Editable. html#delete (int, int).

A `Button` can be added into a layout resource using the `Button` XML tag, as shown in Listing 5-28. The `Button` is a subclass of the `TextView` class. All relevant XML attributes of a `TextView` also apply to a `Button`.

Listing 5-28. Adding the Button into a Layout Resource

```
<Button
    android:id="@+id/button"
    android:layout_width="wrap_content"
    android:layout_height="wrap_content"
    android:drawableLeft="@android:drawable/ic_media_play"
    android:text="Play" />
```

Handling Button Click Events

The `Button` click events get delivered to the application through the `OnClickListener`[49] interface. An instance of `OnClickListener` can be registered with the `Button` instance through the `setOnClickListener`[50] method, as shown in Listing 5-29.

Listing 5-29. Handling the Button Click Event

```
Button button = (Button) findViewById(R.id.button);
button.setOnClickListener(new View.OnClickListener() {
    @Override
    public void onClick(View v) {
        // Button clicked
    }
});
```

ImageButton

There are different flavors of a `Button` control. The `ImageButton`[51] is a `Button` control with an image instead of a text. It can be added to a layout resource through the `ImageButton` XML tag. It takes the drawable image through its `android:src`[52] XML attribute, as shown in Listing 5-30.

---

[49]http://developer.android.com/reference/android/view/View
.OnClickListener. html.
[50]http://developer.android.com/reference/android/view/View
.html#setOnClick Listener(android.view.View.OnClickListener).
[51]http://developer.android.com/reference/android/widget/ImageButton.html.
[52]http://developer.android.com/reference/android/widget/ImageView.html
#attr_android:src.

Listing 5-30. Adding the ImageButton to a Layout Resource

```
<ImageButton
    android:id="@+id/button"
    android:layout_width="wrap_content"
    android:layout_height="wrap_content"
    android:src="@android:drawable/ic_media_play" />
```

Surprisingly, the ImageButton is not a subclass of the Button class as you would expect. It is instead a subclass of the ImageView class. All XML attributes supported by the ImageView also apply to the ImageButton, such as the scaling and tinting.

Although they are not a subclass of the Button class, the click events on an ImageButton are still received through the OnClickListener interface that is registered through the setOnClickListener[53] method of the ImageButton class.

ToggleButton, Switch, and CheckBox

The ToggleButton,[54] Switch,[55] and CheckBox[56] allow the user to change a setting between two states, such as "on" and "off." Although all of these controls fundamentally do the same thing, they provide different visual interfaces to suit different use cases. As shown in Figure 5-11, the ToggleButton has a button-like look and feel, the Switch is a slider-based control, and the CheckBox has simply a check mark next to the text.

Figure 5-11. ToggleButton, Switch, and CheckBox controls in both states

---

[53]http://developer.android.com/reference/android/view/View.
html#setOnClick Listener(android.view.View.OnClickListener).
[54]http://developer.android.com/reference/android/widget/ToggleButton.html.
[55]http://developer.android.com/reference/android/widget/Switch.html.
[56]http://developer.android.com/reference/android/widget/CheckBox.html.

ToggleButton

A `ToggleButton` can be added into a layout resource through the `ToggleButton` XML tag, as shown in Listing 5-31.

Listing 5-31. Adding the ToggleButton into a Layout Resource

```
<ToggleButton
    android:id="@+id/toggle1"
    android:layout_width="wrap_content"
    android:layout_height="wrap_content"
    android:textOff="Off"
    android:textOn="On"
    android:checked="true" />
```

Besides the XML attributes that are supported by the `Button` XML tag, the `ToggleButton` also supports the following attributes:

- ▓ `android:disabledAlpha`: The alpha to apply to the indicator when disabled.

- ▓ `android:textOff`: Text to show when not checked.

- ▓ `android:textOn`: Text to show when checked.

- ▓ `android:checked`: Toggled or not.

Switch

A `Switch` can be added into a layout resource through the `Switch` XML tag, as shown in Listing 5-32.

Listing 5-32. Adding the Switch into a Layout Resource

```
<Switch
    android:id="@+id/toggle3"
    android:layout_width="wrap_content"
    android:layout_height="wrap_content"
    android:textOff="Off"
    android:textOn="On"
    android:checked="true"
    android:showText="true" />
```

Besides the XML attributes that are supported by the `Button` XML tag, the `Switch` also supports additional attributes; the frequently used ones are

- ▓ `android:showText`: Show the text or not.

- ▓ `android:textOff`: Text to show when not checked.

- ▓ `android:textOn`: Text to show when checked.

- android:checked: Switched or not.

- android:thumb: Drawable to use as the thumb.

- android:track: Drawable to use as the track.

CheckBox

A CheckBox can be added into a layout resource through the CheckBox XML tag, as shown in Listing 5-33.

Listing 5-33. Adding the CheckBox into a Layout Resource

```
<CheckBox
    android:id="@+id/toggle5"
    android:layout_width="wrap_content"
    android:layout_height="wrap_content"
    android:text="On"
    android:checked="true" />
```

As the CheckBox is a subclass of the Button class, it supports all the XML attributes supported by the Button class, as well as the following attribute:

- android:checked: Checked or not.

Getting the Checked State

The current state of each of those controls can be queried through the isChecked[57] method, as shown in Listing 5-34.

Listing 5-34. Checking If the Control Is in Checked State

```
if (checkBox.isChecked()) {
    // On state
} else {
    // Off state
}
```

---

[57]http://developer.android.com/reference/android/widget/Checkable.html#isChecked().

Getting Notified on Checked State Change

The application can register an instance of the OnCheckedChangeListener[58] interface through the setOnCheckedChangeListener[59] method to receive a notification when the checked state of the control changes as a result of a user event, as shown in Listing 5-35.

Listing 5-35. Getting Notified on Checked State Change

```
checkBox.setOnCheckedChangeListener(
        new CompoundButton.OnCheckedChangeListener() {
    @Override
    public void onCheckedChanged(
            CompoundButton buttonView,
            boolean isChecked) {
        if (isChecked) {
            // On state
        } else {
            // Off state
        }
    }
});
```

Radio Button

In certain cases, having only two states is not enough to provide a full set of options. The Android framework provides the RadioButton[60] for that purpose. When RadioButtons are combined through a RadioGroup,[61] they can allow the user to select one option from a set of options, as shown in Figure 5-12.

---

[58]http://developer.android.com/reference/android/widget/CompoundButton. OnCheckedChangeListener.html.

[59]http://developer.android.com/reference/android/widget/CompoundButton. html #setOnCheckedChangeListener(android.widget.CompoundButton. OnCheckedChange Listener).

[60]http://developer.android.com/reference/android/widget/RadioButton.html.

[61]http://developer.android.com/reference/android/widget/RadioGroup.html.

Figure 5-12. RadioButtons in a RadioGroup presenting four selections

Note   Another way to prompt the user to select one option from a set of options is to use the `Spinner`, which is covered in the section "Adapter View Layout."

The `RadioButton`, and the `RadioGroup` can be added into a layout resource using the corresponding XML tags, as shown in Listing 5-36.

Listing 5-36. Adding the RadioGroup and the RadioButtons into a Layout Resource

```
<RadioGroup
    android:layout_width="wrap_content"
    android:layout_height="wrap_content">

    <RadioButton
        android:id="@+id/email"
        android:layout_width="wrap_content"
        android:layout_height="wrap_content"
        android:text="E-Mail"
        android:checked="true" />

    <RadioButton
        android:id="@+id/phone"
        android:layout_width="wrap_content"
        android:layout_height="wrap_content"
        android:text="Phone"/>

    <RadioButton
        android:id="@+id/both"
        android:layout_width="wrap_content"
```

```
        android:layout_height="wrap_content"
        android:text="Both"/>

    <RadioButton
        android:id="@+id/none"
        android:layout_width="wrap_content"
        android:layout_height="wrap_content"
        android:text="None"/>

</RadioGroup>
```

As the RadioButton is a subclass of the Button class, it accepts all of the XML attributes of the Button class, with the addition of the android:checked attribute defining whether the RadioButton should be in a checked state by default.

Getting Notified on RadioButton Checked Change

The change events get delivered to the application through the OnCheckedChangeListener[62] interface. An application can register an instance of the OnCheckedChangeListener interface through the setOnCheckedChangeListener[63] method of the RadioGroup, as shown in Listing 5-37.

Listing 5-37. Getting Notified on RadioButton Checked Change

```
radioGroup.setOnCheckedChangeListener(
        new RadioGroup.OnCheckedChangeListener() {
    @Override
    public void onCheckedChanged(
            RadioGroup group,
            int checkedId) {
        switch (checkedId) {
            case R.id.email:
                break;

            case R.id.phone:
                break;
```

---

[62]http://developer.android.com/reference/android/widget/RadioGroup. OnChecked ChangeListener.html.
[63]http://developer.android.com/reference/android/widget/RadioGroup. html#set OnCheckedChangeListener(android.widget.RadioGroup. OnCheckedChangeListener).

```
            case R.id.both:
                break;

            case R.id.none:
                break;
        }
    }
});
```

Fragments

On the Android platform, portions of the user interface can be grouped as modular sections, which have their own life cycle and event handling. These sections are known as fragments, and they are embodied with the Fragment[64] class in Android applications.

Fragments promote reuse of the user interface and also application behavior. Multiple fragments can be combined within a single activity. With the arrival of tablet devices, Android introduced fragments in API Level 11, primarily to support dynamic UI designs. Applications can divide the user interface into modular and reusable components through fragments, and based on screen size and device orientation, the application can structure those accordingly using a proper layout. This enables the same application code to support various screen sizes and orientations.

Creating a Fragment

You can create a fragment by simply extending the Fragment class, as shown in Listing 5-38.

Listing 5-38. Creating a New Fragment by Extending the Fragment Class

```
import android.app.Fragment;

public class ExampleFragment extends Fragment {

}
```

---

[64]http://developer.android.com/reference/android/app/Fragment.html.

Similar to other Android components like the activity, a fragment has its own life cycle. Fragment life-cycle events get delivered to the application through a set of callback methods that can be overridden by the application code to do the appropriate handling.

- onAttach:[65] Called when a fragment is first attached to its activity.

- onCreate:[66] Called after onAttach for the fragment to do initial creation. At this time the activity may not be fully created.

- onCreateView:[67] Called for the fragment to instantiate and return its user interface as a View instance. Fragments without a user interface can simply return null here.

- onActivityCreated:[68] Called when the activity hosting the fragment is fully created and its view hierarchy is instantiated.

- onStart:[69] Called when the fragment is visible to the user.

- onResume:[70] Called when the fragment is visible and actively running.

- onPause:[71] Called when the fragment is no longer visible and active.

---

[65]http://developer.android.com/reference/android/app/Fragment. html#onAttach (android.app.Activity).
[66]http://developer.android.com/reference/android/app/Fragment. html#onCreate (android.os.Bundle).
[67]http://developer.android.com/reference/android/app/Fragment.html# onCreateView(android.view.LayoutInflater, android.view.ViewGroup, android.os.Bundle).
[68]http://developer.android.com/reference/android/app/Fragment.html#on ActivityCreated(android.os.Bundle).
[69]http://developer.android.com/reference/android/app/Fragment.html# onStart().
[70]http://developer.android.com/reference/android/app/Fragment.html# onResume().
[71]http://developer.android.com/reference/android/app/Fragment.html# onPause().

 ▦   onDestroyView:[72] Called when the fragment's view is
      now being detached from the fragment and currently
      getting destroyed.

 ▦   onDestroy:[73] Called when the fragment is no longer in
      use, and getting destroyed.

 ▦   onDetach:[74] Called when the fragment is no longer
      attached to the activity.

Most Android applications are expected to override at least the onCreate,
onCreateView, and onPause methods. During the onPause method, the
fragment can persist its state, as it may never become visible after this call.

Adding a Fragment to an Activity

The application can add a fragment either through the layout file or
programmatically through the provided API.

Adding a Fragment to an Activity Through the Layout

The <fragment> XML tag is supported in the layout files for adding fragments
directly as part of the layout file. The name attribute of the <fragment> XML
tag must be set to the fully qualified name of the fragment class, as shown
in Listing 5-39.

Listing 5-39. Adding a Fragment Through the Layout

```
<fragment
    android:id="@+id/example_fragment"
    android:name="com.apress.chapter5.ExampleFragment"
    android:layout_width="match_parent"
    android:layout_height="match_parent" />
```

---

[72]http://developer.android.com/reference/android/app/Fragment.
html#onDestroy View().
[73]http://developer.android.com/reference/android/app/Fragment.
html#onDestroy ().
[74]http://developer.android.com/reference/android/app/Fragment.
html#onDetach ().

Adding a Fragment to an Activity Programmatically

During the runtime, the application can add a fragment programmatically through the API provided by the FragmentManager[75] class, by simply specifying a view group in which to place the fragment.

Adding a Placeholder into the Layout for the Fragment

As shown in Listing 5-40, the FrameLayout can be used inside the layout file as a placeholder view group for a fragment.

Listing 5-40. The FrameLayout Used as a Placeholder for the Fragment Inside the Layout File

```
<FrameLayout
    android:id="@+id/fragment_container"
    android:layout_width="match_parent"
    android:layout_height="match_parent" />
```

Getting the FragmentManager Instance

The singleton instance of the FragmentManager class can be obtained from the Activity through its getFragmentManager[76] method, as shown in Listing 5-41.

Listing 5-41. Getting the FragmentManager Singleton Instance from the Activity

```
FragmentManager fragmentManager = getFragmentManager();
```

Creating a Fragment Transaction

Fragment-related operations are handled through the API provided by the FragmentTransaction[77] class. A new fragment transaction can be started using the beginTransaction[78] method of the FragmentManager as shown in Listing 5-42.

---

[75]http://developer.android.com/reference/android/app/FragmentManager.html.
[76]http://developer.android.com/reference/android/app/Activity.html#get FragmentManager().
[77]http://developer.android.com/reference/android/app/ FragmentTransaction. html.
[78]http://developer.android.com/reference/android/app/FragmentManager. html# beginTransaction().

Listing 5-42. Creating a Fragment Transaction

```
FragmentTransaction fragmentTransaction =
        fragmentManager.beginTransaction();
```

Adding the Fragment into the Placeholder

The FragmentTransaction class provides a set of APIs to do various fragment-related operations. The add[79] method allows adding a fragment into the specified view group. Multiple transaction operations can occur within a single fragment transaction. The application should call the commit[80] method of the FragmantTransaction object in order to execute the specified the operations, as shown in Listing 5-43.

Listing 5-43. Adding the Fragment into the Given Placeholder View Group

```
fragmentTransaction.add(R.id.fragment_container,
        exampleFragment);

fragmentTransaction.commit();
```

Replacing a Fragment

The FragmentTransaction class also provides methods to manipulate the fragments while the application is running. The replace[81] method allows the application to replace an existing Fragment in a container with a new one, as shown in Listing 5-44.

Listing 5-44. Replacing the existing Fragment with the given Fragment.

```
fragmentTransaction.replace(R.id.fragment_container,
        exampleFragment);
```

Managing the Fragment Back Stack

As the application can add and replace fragments anytime, a single Activity can provide multiple user interfaces by simply shuffling the fragments. As the user cannot be aware of the internals of the application, the expectation is that the Back key on the device should take the user back to the previous screen, which can either be an Activity or a Fragment.

---

[79]http://developer.android.com/reference/android/app/
FragmentTransaction. html#add(int, android.app.Fragment).
[80]http://developer.android.com/reference/android/app/
FragmentTransaction. html#commit().
[81]http://developer.android.com/reference/android/app/
FragmentTransaction.html#replace(int, android.app.Fragment).

Adding a Fragment Transaction to the Back Stack

The FragmentManager provides a fragment back stack for this purpose. As shown in Listing 5-45, using the addToBackStack[82] method of the FragmentTransaction class, the application can inform the FragmentManager that the transaction should be added to the fragment back stack.

Listing 5-45. Adding a FragmentTransaction to the Back Stack

```
fragmentTransaction.addToBackStack(null);
```

Going Backward Using the Back Stack

The popBackStack[83] method of the FragmentManager class can be used to pop the top state off the back stack, as shown in Listing 5-46.

> **Note**   The popBackStack method puts the previous FragmentTransaction in the queue and returns immediately. It does not perform the actual operation. The application should not assume that the previous Fragment is visible.

Listing 5-46. Going Backward Using the Fragment Back Stack

```
fragmentManager.popBackStack();
```

Adding a User Interface to a Fragment

By overriding the onCreateView method, the fragment can return a View instance in order to provide a user interface. As shown in Listing 5-47, the fragment can utilize the provided LayoutInflater instance to inflate its user interface layout.

---

[82]http://developer.android.com/reference/android/app/
FragmentTransaction. html#addToBackStack(java.lang.String).
[83]http://developer.android.com/reference/android/app/FragmentManager.
html# popBackStack().

Listing 5-47. Inflating the User Interface Layout of a Fragment

```
@Override
public View onCreateView(LayoutInflater inflater,
                         ViewGroup container,
                         Bundle savedInstanceState) {
    return inflater.inflate(R.layout.fragment_example,
            container, false);
}
```

Passing Arguments to a Fragment

As fragments are reusable components, they can be utilized in various places within an application. For a fragment to provide the proper functionality based on the current context, the application may need to provide certain arguments to the fragment. This is achieved through the setArguments[84] method of the Fragment class. As shown in Listing 5-48, the setArguments method takes a Bundle instance containing the arguments as key and value pairs.

> **Note**   We recommend using the setArguments method, instead of
> directly manipulating a Fragment instance. The Android framework
> provides the same arguments to the fragment, if the fragment was
> destroyed and recreated by the framework.

Listing 5-48. Passing Arguments to a Fragment

```
Bundle arguments = new Bundle();
arguments.putString("name", "Onur Cinar");
arguments.putBoolean("showLink", false);

ExampleFragment exampleFragment = new ExampleFragment();
exampleFragment.setArguments(arguments);
```

---

[84]http://developer.android.com/reference/android/app/Fragment.html#set
Arguments(android.os.Bundle).

Using the Arguments in a Fragment

The fragment can access the passed fragments using the getArguments[85]
method of the Fragment class, as shown in Listing 5-49.

Listing 5-49. Accessing the Passed Arguments in a Fragment

```java
public class ExampleFragment extends Fragment {
    @Override
    public void onCreate(Bundle savedInstanceState) {
        super.onCreate(savedInstanceState);

        Bundle arguments = getArguments();
        if (arguments != null) {
            String name = arguments.getString(
                    "name", "Default Name");

            boolean showLink = arguments.getBoolean(
                    "showLink", false);
        }
    }
}
```

Communication Between the Activity and the Fragment

Both the Fragment and the Activity can access each other and exchange
information while the application is running. This makes it possible to group
portions of the user interface as modular and reusable components but still
deliver a smooth user interface.

Accessing the Activity from the Fragment

The Fragment can access the hosting Activity instance using the
getActivity[86] method of the Fragment class, as shown in Listing 5-50.

---

[85]http://developer.android.com/reference/android/app/Fragment.html#get
Arguments().
[86]http://developer.android.com/reference/android/app/Fragment.html#get
Activity().

Listing 5-50. Getting the Activity Instance from the Fragment

```
MainActivity mainActivity = (MainActivity) getActivity();
```

Accessing the Fragment from the Activity

Once the Fragment instance is added to the Activity, it can be accessed through the findFragmentById[87] method of the FragmentManager class, as shown in Listing 5-51.

Listing 5-51. Getting the Fragment Instance from the Activity

```
ExampleFragment exampleFragment =
        (ExampleFragment) fragmentManager.findFragmentById(
                R.id.example_fragment);
```

Summary

This chapter provided a brief overview of the APIs provided by the Android framework for developing extensive user interfaces on the Android platform. As the Android ecosystem is highly fragmented due to various display sizes and densities, the chapter started by exploring the various layout types that are provided by the Android framework in order to provide a fluid user interface that can adapt to any display size. The chapter also gave an overview of the input and output controls provided by the Android framework. The Fragment API was introduced at last, to allow the parts of a user interface to be broken down into modular and reusable pieces that can be used in different parts of the application.

---

[87]http://developer.android.com/reference/android/app/FragmentManager.html# findFragmentById(int).

Chapter 6

User Interface

Although every Android application runs as a full-screen application, the Android platform still provides a certain amount of window features, such as the action bar, toasts, dialogs, and notifications. This chapter provides a brief overview of these fundamental window features. Although not every Android application benefits from toasts and dialogs, the action bar and notifications are frequently used by almost every Android application to provide a smooth and consistent user experience.

Action Bar

Through the action bar,[1] the Android platform provides window features to help the user to easily identify the running application, his location within the application, important application actions, and navigation options.

> **Note** The three vertical dots icon on the right-hand side of the action bar is known as the overflow menu. Once it gets a click event, it shows a drop-down menu with a list of actions that are not displayed directly on the action bar.

---

[1]http://developer.android.com/reference/android/app/ActionBar.html.

As shown in Figure 6-1, the action bar consists of

- The application's icon and title.

- Icons and labels of important application actions, and an overflow menu if the entire list of actions cannot be displayed on the action bar due to the amount of available space.

- Navigation support within the application through the back button, tabs, and drop-down menus.

Figure 6-1. The action bar and its components

Adding the Action Bar

The action bar application programming interface (API) was first introduced in API Level 11, but it is also available for earlier API levels through the Android Support Library. Starting with API Level 11, the ActionBar is included in all activities using the default Theme.Holo theme. The application can access the ActionBar instance anytime through the getActionBar[2] method of the Activity class, as shown in Listing 6-1.

Listing 6-1. Getting the ActionBar Instance from the Activity

```
ActionBar actionBar = getActionBar();
```

---

[2]http://developer.android.com/reference/android/app/Activity.html #getActionBar().

Removing the Action Bar

As the `ActionBar` instance is included by default starting from API Level 11 and beyond, the application can simply remote it using its hide[3] method if it is not needed, as shown in Listing 6-2.

Listing 6-2. Removing the Action Bar

```
@Override
protected void onCreate(Bundle savedInstanceState) {
    ActionBar actionBar = getActionBar();
    actionBar.hide();
}
```

Adding Actions to the Action Bar

The action bar provides a prominent place to show important application actions related to the current context. These actions are displayed on the action bar with an icon and sometimes with both an icon and text based on how it gets declared.

Defining the Actions for the Action Bar

The actions are defined as a menu resource in the `res/menu` resource directory, as shown in Listing 6-3.

Listing 6-3. The Content of res/menu/menu_actions.xml File

```
<menu xmlns:android=
        "http://schemas.android.com/apk/res/android">

    <item
        android:id="@+id/action_search"
        android:title="@string/action_search"
        android:icon="@drawable/ic_action_search" />

    <item
        android:id="@+id/action_save"
        android:title="@string/action_save"
        android:icon="@drawable/ic_action_save" />
```

---

[3]http://developer.android.com/reference/android/app/ActionBar.
html#hide().

```
<item android:id="@+id/action_share"
    android:title="@string/action_share"
    android:icon="@drawable/ic_action_share" />

<item android:id="@+id/action_settings"
    android:title="@string/action_settings"
    android:icon="@drawable/ic_action_settings"
    android:showAsAction="never" />

<item android:id="@+id/action_about"
    android:title="@string/action_about"
    android:icon="@drawable/ic_action_about"
    android:showAsAction="never" />
</menu>
```

Each action gets defined through the `<item>`[4] XML tag, with an ID, an icon, and a title. The `<item>` tag can also take additional parameters that will define how the action should be displayed on the action bar.

Controlling the Appearance of Action Items

As the screen space is a scarce resource on mobile devices, if the actions cannot all fit into the action bar, they get placed in an overflow menu (see Figure 6-1). As shown in Listing 6-4, through the `showAsAction` parameter of the `<item>` tag, the application can provide a hint to the Android framework on how the action should be displayed.

- `ifRoom`: Only place this action in the action bar if there is enough room; otherwise, place it in the overflow menu.

- `never`: Never place this action in the action bar, always place it in the overflow menu.

- `withText`: Include text title for the action item.

- `always`: Always place this action in the action bar.

- `collapseActionView`: Collapse the action item if supported.

---

[4]http://developer.android.com/guide/topics/resources/menu-resource.html#item-element.

> **Caution**   It is recommended to use ifRoom instead of always. Android device form factors are highly fragmented, and it is better to let the Android platform make the proper judgment about how many actions should be placed in the action bar.

Listing 6-4. Controlling the Appearance of Action Items Using showAsAction Parameter

```
<item
    android:id="@+id/action_search"
    android:title="@string/action_search"
    android:icon="@drawable/ic_action_search"
    android:showAsAction="ifRoom|collapseActionView"/>
```

Displaying the Actions in the Action Bar

For the defined action bar items to be displayed in the action bar, they need to be inflated as a Menu[5] instance. This should be done by overriding the onCreateOptionsMenu[6] method of the Activity class, as shown in Listing 6-5. The Android framework will call this method when the action bar is getting displayed.

Listing 6-5. Inflating the Actions to the Action Bar

```
@Override
public boolean onCreateOptionsMenu(Menu menu) {
    getMenuInflater().inflate(R.menu.menu_actions, menu);
    return true;
}
```

Handling Clicks on Actions

The click events from the action bar get delivered to the application through the onOptionsItemSelected[7] method of the Activity class. As shown in Listing 6-6, the onOptionsItemSelected method gets called with the

---

[5]http://developer.android.com/reference/android/view/Menu.html.
[6]http://developer.android.com/reference/android/app/Activity.html #onCreateOptionsMenu(android.view.Menu).
[7]http://developer.android.com/reference/android/app/Activity.html #onOptionsItemSelected(android.view.MenuItem).

MenuItem[8] instance for the selected action. The application can then extract the item ID through the getItemId method to identify which action gets selected. If the click event got processed, the application is expected to return true to inform the Android platform.

Listing 6-6. Handling the Action Selection

```
@Override
public boolean onOptionsItemSelected(MenuItem item) {
    boolean consumed = true;

    switch (item.getItemId()) {
        case R.id.action_save:
            break;

        case R.id.action_share:
            break;

        default:
            consumed = super.onOptionsItemSelected(item);
    }

    return consumed;
}
```

In addition to the onOptionsItemSelected, the application can also use the android:onClick attribute of the item XML tag in the menu resource to specify a callback method to handle click events for individual actions, as shown in Listing 6-7.

Listing 6-7. Declaring a Callback Method to Handle the Click Event

```
<item
    android:id="@+id/action_save"
    android:title="@string/action_save"
    android:icon="@drawable/ic_action_save"
    android:showAsAction="ifRoom"
    android:onClick="save"/>
```

Once the action is clicked, the save method of the Activity instance will be invoked to handle the event, as shown in Listing 6-8.

---

[8]http://developer.android.com/reference/android/view/MenuItem.html.

Listing 6-8. The Callback Method in the Activity Class

```
public void save(MenuItem item) {
    // Handle action click event
}
```

Action Views

Regular actions get displayed as an icon on the action bar, and the application is expected to present access to the actual action as a result of the user clicking on the action icon. In order to provide faster access to the actions, Android provides action views. Action views are widgets that appear on the action bar as a substitute for action icons. Action view widgets give direct access to actions without the extra step. As shown in Figure 6-2, the SearchView[9] instance is a good example of the action view.

Figure 6-2. *SearchView on the action bar*

SearchView allows the user to start the search action immediately from the action bar.

Adding Action Views to the Action Bar

Action views are also declared through the actionViewClass attribute of the <item> tag, as shown in Listing 6-9.

Listing 6-9. Declaring an Action with an Action View

```
<item
    android:id="@+id/action_search"
    android:title="@string/action_search"
    android:icon="@drawable/ic_action_search"
    android:showAsAction="ifRoom "
    android:actionViewClass="android.widget.SearchView"/>
```

---

[9]http://developer.android.com/reference/android/widget/SearchView.html.

Action views can be a View, or they can be a view layout. The actionLayout attribute can be used instead of the actionViewClass attribute if a layout will be used for the action view.

Accessing the Action View Instance

The application can access the instance of the action view within the onCreateOptionsMenu method after inflating the menu resource, as shown in Listing 6-10.

Listing 6-10. Accessing the Action View Instance

```
@Override
public boolean onCreateOptionsMenu(Menu menu) {
    getMenuInflater().inflate(R.menu.menu_main, menu);

    MenuItem searchMenuItem =
            menu.findItem(R.id.action_search);
    SearchView searchView =
            (SearchView) searchMenuItem.getActionView();

    return true;
}
```

Collapsing Action Views to Preserve Space

As shown in Figure 6-2, action views, by their nature, can take up a large portion of the action bar. As shown in Listing 6-11, the application can use the collapseActionView in the showAsAction attribute to provide a hint to the Android platform that the action view should be collapsed into an action button.

Listing 6-11. Collapsing an Action View

```
<item
    android:id="@+id/action_search"
    android:title="@string/action_search"
    android:icon="@drawable/ic_action_search"
    android:showAsAction="ifRoom|collapseActionView"
    android:actionViewClass="android.widget.SearchView"/>
```

As shown in Figure 6-3, the Android platform is handling the collapse operation; the application does not have handle the click event for the action. It will automatically get expanded to show the action view.

Figure 6-3. Collapsed action view shown as a button

Action Providers

Although action views allow replacing action buttons with rich widgets, they do not automatically handle the actual action that the widget should perform. The Android framework delivers action providers to fill this gap. Action providers, besides replacing the action button with a custom layout, also take full control of all the action's behaviors.

The ShareActionProvider is a good example of action providers. As shown in Figure 6-4, the ShareActionProvider replaces the action button with a drop-down menu listing all possible ways that the content can be shared.

Figure 6-4. ShareActionProvider with a drop-down menu

Besides rendering the list, it also handles the internals of sharing the content per the user's selection.

Adding the Action Provider to the Action Bar

Action views are also declared through the actionProviderClass attribute of the <item> tag, as shown in Listing 6-12.

Listing 6-12. Adding the Share Action Provider to the Action Bar

```
<item android:id="@+id/action_share"
    android:title="@string/action_share"
    android:showAsAction="ifRoom"
    android:actionProviderClass=
        "android.widget.ShareActionProvider"/>
```

Initializing the Action Provider

As the action provider needs to perform a certain operation, it may require some additional information from the application. As shown in Listing 6-13, the application can initialize action providers within the onCreateOptionsMenu method of the Activity class.

Listing 6-13. Initializing the Action Provider

```
@Override
public boolean onCreateOptionsMenu(Menu menu) {
    getMenuInflater().inflate(R.menu.menu_toast, menu);

    MenuItem menuItem = menu.findItem(R.id.action_share);
    ShareActionProvider shareActionProvider =
            (ShareActionProvider) menuItem.getActionProvider();

    Intent intent = new Intent(Intent.ACTION_SEND);
    intent.setType("image/*");

    shareActionProvider.setShareIntent(intent);
    return true;
}
```

Toasts

Toast is a small pop-up window that provides feedback to the user about an application operation. Toast provides feedback as the Toast[10] class in the Android framework. Toasts are displayed for a short period of time and disappear. Toasts are information-only pop-up windows; they cannot interact with the user, as shown in Figure 6-5.

---

[10]http://developer.android.com/reference/android/widget/Toast.html.

Figure 6-5. *Toast message*

The application can show a toast message anytime by creating the toast using the makeText[11] method of the Toast class and then calling its show[12] method, as shown in Listing 6-14.

Listing 6-14. *Displaying a Toast Message*

```
Toast toast = Toast.makeText(this,
        "Message Sent",
        Toast.LENGTH_SHORT);

toast.show();
```

The makeText method takes the current context, the message to display, and the toast duration. The message can be supplied as a simple string or a string resource ID. The Toast class provides two constants for the supported toast durations.

- LENGTH_SHORT: Toast message for a short period of time.

- LENGTH_LONG: Toast message for a long period of time.

> **Note**   As a best practice, toasts should only be used when the application is in the foreground. When the application is backgrounded, any feedback from the application should be delivered to the user through notifications rather than toasts.

---

[11]http://developer.android.com/reference/android/widget/Toast.html#makeText(android.content.Context, int, int).
[12]http://developer.android.com/reference/android/widget/Toast.html#show().

Dialogs

Toast messages are informational only; they cannot receive the user's input. If the application needs to prompt for the user's input, the Android framework provides dialog messages. Similar to toasts, dialogs are also small pop-up windows that do not fill the screen. Dialogs can contain variety of input controls to interact with the user. On the Android platform, dialogs are implemented on top of the Dialog[13] base class.

Dialog Flavors

In order to facilitate the usage of dialog messages, the Android platform also provides dialog flavors for most common use cases, such as the alert dialog, the date picker dialog, the progress dialog, the time picker dialog, the character picker dialog, the media route chooser dialer, and the media route controller dialog. Applications can easily customize these dialogs to fit unique application needs.

> **Caution**   We recommend that developers customize these dialog flavors instead of directly building a new dialog on top of the Dialog base class.

Alert Dialog

Alert dialogs are provided through the AlertDialog[14] class. This is the most generic dialog flavor provided by the Android framework. All variety of dialogs can be built on top of the alert dialogs. As shown in Figure 6-6, an alert dialog consists of three parts.

- **Title:** An optional dialog title.
- **Content:** A message, a list, or other custom layout.
- **Buttons:** Up to three action buttons for the dialog.

---

[13]http://developer.android.com/reference/android/app/Dialog.html.
[14]http://developer.android.com/reference/android/app/AlertDialog.html.

Figure 6-6. Alert dialog

Creating an Alert Dialog

An alert dialog can be created using the AlertDialog.Builder[15] builder class, as shown in Listing 6-15.

Listing 6-15. Creating an Alert Dialog Using the Alert Dialog Builder

```
AlertDialog alertDialog = new AlertDialog.Builder(this)
        .setTitle("Dialog Title")
        .setMessage("Do you want to save?")
        .create();
```

The setMessage[16] method of AlertDialog.Builder populates the content area of the alert dialog with the given message text. Both the setTitle[17] method and the setMessage method accept the text as a string, or as a string resource. Calling the create[18] method creates an AlertDialog instance.

---

[15]http://developer.android.com/reference/android/app/AlertDialog.
Builder.html.

[16]http://developer.android.com/reference/android/app/AlertDialog.
Builder.html#setMessage(java.lang.CharSequence).

[17]http://developer.android.com/reference/android/app/AlertDialog.
Builder.html#setTitle(java.lang.CharSequence).

[18]http://developer.android.com/reference/android/app/AlertDialog.
Builder.html#create().

Adding Buttons to an Alert Dialog

The alert dialog supports up to three buttons: the positive button, the negative button, and the neutral button.

(1) Adding the Positive Button

The positive button is used to for the accept action, such as the "OK" button. The setPositiveButton[19] method of the AlertDialog.Builder is used to define the positive button, as shown in Listing 6-16.

Listing 6-16. Adding the Positive Button to the Alert Dialog

```
AlertDialog alertDialog = new AlertDialog.Builder(this)
        .setTitle("Dialog Title")
        .setMessage("Do you want to save your changes?")
        .setPositiveButton("Save",
                new DialogInterface.OnClickListener() {
            @Override
            public void onClick(
                    DialogInterface dialogInterface,
                    int which) {
                // Save the user's changes.
            }
        })
        .create();
}
```

The setPositiveButton method takes the button's label and a DialogInterface.OnClickListener[20] interface implementation to handle the click action.

Tip   The DialogInterface.OnClickListener's onClick[21] callback method takes the button type as its last parameter. Instead of providing multiple implementations of this interface, the application may choose to provide a single implementation, and use the button-type parameter to detect which button the user clicks.

(2) Adding the Negative Button

The negative button is used for the cancel action. Similar to the positive button, the setNegativeButton[22] method of the AlertDialog.Builder class is used to add the negative button.

(3) Adding the Neutral Button

The neutral button allows the user to skip making a decision, such as clicking the "Remind me later" button. Similar to both positive and negative buttons, the neutral button is also added to the alert dialog through the setNeutralButton[23] method of the AlertDialog.Builder class.

Using a List on an Alert Dialog

Besides these three support button types, the alert dialog can also contain complex input controls, such as a list of items to choose from, as shown in Figure 6-7.

---

[21]http://developer.android.com/reference/android/content/
DialogInterface.OnClickListener.html#onClick(android.content.
DialogInterface, int).
[22]http://developer.android.com/reference/android/app/AlertDialog.
Builder.html#setNegativeButton(java.lang.CharSequence,android.content.
Dialog Interface.OnClickListener).
[23]http://developer.android.com/reference/android/app/AlertDialog.
Builder.html#setNeutralButton(java.lang.CharSequence,android.content.
Dialog Interface.OnClickListener).

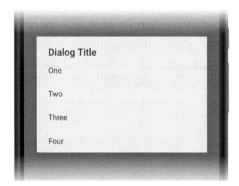

Figure 6-7. *Using a list in the alert dialog*

The setItems[24] method of the AlertDialog.Builder class is used to set the content of such list. The AlertDialog.Builder class provides two flavors of setItems method. The method can either take the list of items from a string array, as shown in Listing 6-15, or, instead, take a string array resource ID.

Listing 6-17. Using a List in the Alert Dialog

```
final String[] items = {
        "One", "Two", "Three", "Four"
};

AlertDialog alertDialog = new AlertDialog.Builder(this)
        .setTitle("Dialog Title")
        .setItems(items,new DialogInterface.OnClickListener() {
            @Override
            public void onClick(
                    DialogInterface dialogInterface,
                    int what) {
                String item = items[what];
            }
        })
        .create();
```

---

[24]http://developer.android.com/reference/android/app/AlertDialog.
Builder.html#setItems(java.lang.CharSequence[],android.content.
DialogInterface.OnClickListener).

The alert dialog notifies the application about the selected item through the provided `DialogInterface.OnClickListener` instance. The `which` parameter of the `onClick` callback method takes the index position of the selected item.

(4) Using a Multi-Choice List in the Alert Dialog

Alert dialogs can also be configured to show either a multi-choice or a single-choice list, as shown in Figure 6-8.

Figure 6-8. Using a multi-choice list in the alert dialog

The `AlertDialog.Builder` class provides the `setMutiChoiceItems`[25] method to configure the alert dialog to render a multi-choice list, as shown in Listing 6-18.

Listing 6-18. Rendering a Multi-choice List in the Alert Dialog Using the setMultiChoiceItems Method

```
final String[] items = {
        "One", "Two", "Three", "Four"
};

final boolean[] checked = {
        false, true, false, false
};
```

---

[25]http://developer.android.com/reference/android/app/AlertDialog.
Builder.html#setMultiChoiceItems(java.lang.CharSequence[], boolean[],
android.content.DialogInterface.OnMultiChoiceClickListener).

```
AlertDialog alertDialog = new AlertDialog.Builder(ToastActivity.this)
        .setTitle("Dialog Title")
        .setMultiChoiceItems(
            items,
            checked,
            new DialogInterface.OnMultiChoiceClickListener() {
                    @Override
                    public void onClick(
                            DialogInterface dialogInterface,
                            int what,
                            boolean isChecked) {

                    }
            }
        )
        .create();
```

The setMultiChoiceItems method takes a string array of list items, an optional Boolean array indicating which items must be checked by default. The list change events get delivered to the application through the DialogInterface.OnMultiChoiceClickListener[26] interface.

(5) Using a Single-Choice List in the Alert Dialog

The setSingleChoiceItems[27] method can be used the same way to render a single-choice list within the alert dialog, as shown in Figure 6-9.

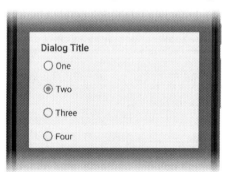

Figure 6-9. Using a single-choice list in the alert dialog

---

[26]http://developer.android.com/reference/android/content/
DialogInterface.OnMultiChoiceClickListener.html.
[27]http://developer.android.com/reference/android/app/AlertDialog.
Builder.html#setSingleChoiceItems(java.lang.CharSequence[], int,
android.content.DialogInterface.OnClickListener).

> **Note**   Both the `setSingleChoiceItems` and the `setItems` provide a
> single-choice list to the user. The advantage of using the single-choice list is
> that it persists the user's choice, so that subsequent access to the same dialog
> will start with the user's previous selection as the default.

The `setSingleChoiceItems` method takes a string array for the list options
and an optional index value for the default selection. The selection
change gets delivered to the application through the `DialogInterface.`
`OnClickListener`, as shown in Listing 6-19.

*Listing 6-19. Rendering a Single-Choice List in the Alert Dialog Using the setSingleChoiceItems
Method*

```
AlertDialog alertDialog = new AlertDialog.Builder(ToastActivity.this)
        .setTitle("Dialog Title")
        .setSingleChoiceItems(
            items,
            1,
            new DialogInterface.OnClickListener() {
                @Override
                public void onClick(
                        DialogInterface dialogInterface,
                        int what) {

                }
            }
        )
        .create();
```

Using a Custom Layout in an Alert Dialog

Besides the provided alert dialog types, through the `setView` method of the
`AlertDialog.Builder` class, the application can also provide its own custom
layout as the content of the alert dialog, as shown in Figure 6-10.

Figure 6-10. Using a custom layout on alert dialog

The setView method takes a custom view instance to fill the alert dialog's content area. The custom view can be defined in a regular layout XML file and then inflated as a view, as shown in Listing 6-20.

Listing 6-20. Rendering a Custom Layout in an Alert Dialog

```
LayoutInflater layoutInflater = getLayoutInflater();
View customDialog = layoutInflater.inflate(
        R.layout.custom_dialog, null);

final RatingBar ratingBar = (RatingBar)
customDialog.findViewById(R.id.ratingBar);

final AlertDialog alertDialog = new AlertDialog.Builder(ToastActivity.this)
        .setTitle("Dialog Title")
        .setView(customDialog)
        .setPositiveButton("OK",
                new DialogInterface.OnClickListener() {
            @Override
            public void onClick(
                    DialogInterface dialogInterface, int i) {
                int numberOfStars = ratingBar.getNumStars();
            }
        })
        .create();
```

Date Picker Dialog

The DatePickerDialog[28] is a simple predefined alert dialog with a DatePicker[29] widget as its content, as shown in Figure 6-11.

---

[28]http://developer.android.com/reference/android/app/DatePickerDialog.html.
[29]http://developer.android.com/reference/android/widget/DatePicker.html.

Figure 6-11. DatePickerDialog prompting the user for a date

It can easily be used by applications to prompt the user for a date selection. As shown in Listing 6-21, the DatePickerDialog, takes the current activity context, a DatePickerDialog.OnDateSetListener[30] implementation, and the default values for year, month, and day.

Listing 6-21. DatePickerDialog Initialization

```
DatePickerDialog datePickerDialog = new DatePickerDialog(
        getActivity(),
        new DatePickerDialog.OnDateSetListener() {
            @Override
            public void onDateSet(DatePicker datePicker,
                            int year,
                            int monthOfYear,
                            int dayOfMonth) {

        }
    },
```

---

[30]http://developer.android.com/reference/android/app/DatePickerDialog. OnDateSetListener.html.

```
            calendar.get(Calendar.YEAR),
            calendar.get(Calendar.MONTH),
            calendar.get(Calendar.DAY_OF_MONTH)
);
```

Time Picker Dialog

In the same way, the TimePickerDialog[31] prompts the user to select a time using the TimePicker[32] widget, as shown in Figure 6-12.

Figure 6-12. TimePickerDialog prompting user for time

The TimePickerDialog takes the current activity context, a TimePickerDialog.OnSetTimeListener[33] instance, the default hour and minute, and whether to use a 24-hour view, as shown in Listing 6-22.

---

[31]http://developer.android.com/reference/android/app/TimePickerDialog.html.
[32]http://developer.android.com/reference/android/widget/TimePicker.html.
[33]http://developer.android.com/reference/android/app/TimePickerDialog.
OnTimeSetListener.html.

Listing 6-22. TimePickerDialog Initialization

```
TimePickerDialog timePickerDialog = new TimePickerDialog(
      getActivity(),
      new TimePickerDialog.OnTimeSetListener() {
          @Override
          public void onTimeSet(
                  TimePicker timePicker,
                  int hour,
                  int minute) {

          }
      },
      calendar.get(Calendar.HOUR),
      calendar.get(Calendar.MINUTE),
      true
);
```

Progress Dialog

The ProgressDialog[34] provides an alert dialog with a ProgressBar[35] widget.
In addition to the progress indicator, it can show a message, as shown in
Figure 6-13.

Figure 6-13. ProgressDialog showing the current progress percentage

The ProgressDialog provides methods to configure the ProgressBar.
As shown in Listing 6-23, through these methods, the ProgressBar style,
maximum value, and current progress can be changed.

---

[34]http://developer.android.com/reference/android/app/ProgressDialog.html.
[35]http://developer.android.com/reference/android/widget/ProgressBar.html.

Listing 6-23. Initializing the ProgressDialog Instance

```
ProgressDialog progressDialog = new ProgressDialog(getActivity());
progressDialog.setProgressStyle(
        ProgressDialog.STYLE_HORIZONTAL);
progressDialog.setTitle("Loading...");
progressDialog.setMessage("http://www.apress.com/file.dat");
progressDialog.setMax(100);
progressDialog.incrementProgressBy(60);
```

Showing a Dialog

Although the Dialog class provides a show method to display the dialog, this method does not handle the necessary life-cycle events directly. Android recommends wrapping the dialogs within a DialogFragment[36] before showing them. The DialogFragment handles the life-cycle events such as the user clicking the back button. As shown in Listing 6-24, the actual dialog needs to be initialized and returned by overriding the onCreateDialog[37] method of DialogFragment.

Listing 6-24. DialogFragment Wrapping an AlertDialog Instance

```
DialogFragment dialogFragment = new DialogFragment() {
    @Override
    public Dialog onCreateDialog(Bundle savedInstanceState) {
        AlertDialog alertDialog =
                new AlertDialog.Builder(getActivity())
                    .setTitle("Dialog Title")
                    .setMessage("Do you want to save?")
                    .create();

        return alertDialog;
    }
};
```

The DialogFragment provides methods to control the dialog and manage its appearance. The dialog can be displayed through the show[38] method, as shown in Listing 6-25.

---

[36]http://developer.android.com/reference/android/app/DialogFragment.html.
[37]http://developer.android.com/reference/android/app/DialogFragment.html#onCreateDialog(android.os.Bundle).
[38]http://developer.android.com/reference/android/app/DialogFragment.html#show(android.app.FragmentManager, java.lang.String).

Listing 6-25. Showing an AlertDialog Using the DialogFragment

```
dialogFragment.show(
        getFragmentManager(),
        "dialog");
```

Notifications

Through the toasts and the dialogs, the application can easily notify the user and prompt for information while the application is in the foreground. When the application is backgrounded, it can communicate with the user through the notifications. Once posted, the notifications appear as an icon in the notification area, as shown in Figure 6-14.

Figure 6-14. Notification icon displayed in the notification area

In order to see the details of the notification, as shown in Figure 6-15, the user can simply expand the notification drawer.

Figure 6-15. Notification expanded in the notification drawer

Accessing the Notification Service

The NotificationManager[39] class provides the Notification API. As shown in Listing 6-26, the application can access the instance of the NotificationManager by requesting the system service through the getSystemService method of the current context and providing the constant NOTIFICATION_SERVICE[40] as the name. The Android platform does not require special permission for applications to access the notification service.

Listing 6-26. Getting the Notification Manager Instance

```
NotificationManager notificationManager =
        (NotificationManager) getSystemService(
                Context.NOTIFICATION_SERVICE);
```

Posting a Notification

Each individual notification is represented through the Notification[41] class. In order to display a notification, Android requires the notification object to contain at least a title, a detail text, and a small icon.

The Notification.Builder[42] class is provided by the Android framework as a convenient way to set various characteristics of a Notification object. As shown in Listing 6-27, after setting the necessary fields, the application can invoke the build[43] method of the Notification.Builder object to build a Notification class instance.

Listing 6-27. Building a Notification Object Through the Notification Builder

```
Notification notification = new Notification.Builder(this)
        .setContentTitle("New Message")
        .setContentText("onur.cinar@gmail.com")
        .setSmallIcon(R.drawable.ic_apress)
        .build();
```

---

[39]http://developer.android.com/reference/android/app/
NotificationManager.html.
[40]http://developer.android.com/reference/android/content/Context.html#
NOTIFICATION_SERVICE.
[41]http://developer.android.com/reference/android/app/Notification.html.
[42]http://developer.android.com/reference/android/app/Notification.
Builder.html.
[43]http://developer.android.com/reference/android/app/Notification.
Builder.html#build().

The notification can then be posted through the notify[44] method of the NotificationManager class, as shown in Listing 6-28. The notify method takes a unique identifier for this notification within the application and a Notification object.

Listing 6-28. Posting a Notification to Be Shown in the Notification Area

```
notificationManager.notify(1, notification);
```

Adding Actions to a Notification

Notifications are expected to provide at least a single action to take the user back to the application once the user clicks the notification. The setContentIntent[45] of the Notification.Builder can be used to set a PendingIntent to be started once the user clicks the notification, as shown in Listing 6-29.

Listing 6-29. Adding a Default Action to a Notification

```
Intent intent = new Intent(this, MessageActivity.class);

PendingIntent pendingIntent = PendingIntent.getActivity(
        this, 0, intent, 0);

Notification notification = new Notification.Builder(this)
        .setContentTitle("New Message")
        .setContentText("onur.cinar@gmail.com")
        .setSmallIcon(R.drawable.ic_apress)
        .setContentIntent(pendingIntent)
        .build();
```

Back Stack

Consistent navigation is essential for a smooth user experience. The Android platform provides a back button to make it easier for the user to navigate backward through the history of screens that he previously visited. The Android platform achieves this by keeping a back stack of all started activities. Although this is automatically handled by the platform most of the time, there are certain exceptions, and notifications are one of them.

---

[44]http://developer.android.com/reference/android/app/ NotificationManager.html#notify(int, android.app.Notification).
[45]http://developer.android.com/reference/android/app/Notification. Builder.html#setContentIntent(android.app.PendingIntent).

Notifications allow the user to enter a deep-level activity directly by clicking the notification. At this time, the deep-level activity starts without a back stack. For example, an e-mail application would normally have an inbox activity with a list of all messages and a message activity to display the content of each message. In case of a new message notification, the user will enter directly into the message activity without going through the inbox activity. In such cases, the application is expected to synthesize a new back stack.

Building the Back Stack

The Android framework provides the TaskStackBuilder[46] class to allow anapplication to build the back stack, as shown in Listing 6-30.

Listing 6-30. Building the Back Stack Using the TaskStackBuilder

```
Intent intent = new Intent(this, ToastActivity.class);

TaskStackBuilder taskStackBuilder =
        TaskStackBuilder.create(this);

taskStackBuilder.addParentStack(MessageActivity.class);
taskStackBuilder.addNextIntent(intent);

PendingIntent pendingIntent =
        taskStackBuilder.getPendingIntent(
                0, PendingIntent.FLAG_UPDATE_CURRENT);
```

The addParentStack[47] method of TaskStackBuilder tries to automatically build the back stack based on the parent hierarchy of the given activity. The parent hierarchy of an activity is declared in the manifest file. The parentActivityName[48] attribute of the <activity> XML tag specifies the parent activity, as shown in Listing 6-31.

---

[46]http://developer.android.com/reference/android/app/TaskStackBuilder.html.
[47]http://developer.android.com/reference/android/app/TaskStackBuilder.html #addParentStack(android.app.Activity).
[48]http://developer.android.com/guide/topics/manifest/activity-element.html#parent.

Listing 6-31. Declaring the Parent Hierarchy of an Activity

```
<activity android:name=".InboxActivity">
</activity>

<activity android:name=".MessageActivity"
    android:parentActivityName=".InboxActivity">

</activity>
```

Adding Action Buttons to a Notification

The Notification API also enables an application to incorporate up to three buttons in the notification for additional actions, as shown in Figure 6-16.

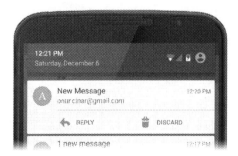

Figure 6-16. Notification with two action buttons

By default, when the notification is collapsed, these action buttons are not visible, and the application is still expected to provide a default action for this case. The addAction[49] method of the Notification.Builder class is used to add action buttons to a notification as shown in Listing 6-32.

---

[49]http://developer.android.com/reference/android/app/Notification.
Builder.html#addAction(int, java.lang.CharSequence, android.app.
PendingIntent).

Listing 6-32. Adding Action Buttons to a Notification

```
Notification notification = new Notification.Builder(this)
        .setContentTitle("New Message")
        .setContentText("onur.cinar@gmail.com")
        .setSmallIcon(R.drawable.ic_apress)
        .setContentIntent(pendingIntent)
        .addAction(R.drawable.ic_action_reply,
                "Reply", replyPendingIntent)
        .addAction(R.drawable.ic_action_discard,
                "Discard", discardPendingIntent)
        .build();
```

Updating a Notification

Once the notification gets displayed, the application can still update it. Using the same unique notification identifier, the application can post a new notification that will replace the previous one. For example, in case of a messaging application, the Notification.InboxStyle[50] can be used to combine the notifications under a single notification, as shown in Figure 6-17.

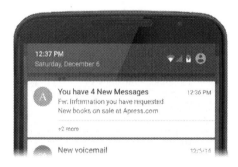

Figure 6-17. Combined notifications using the inbox style

The Android platform can display notifications in an expanded view when a layout is specified through the setStyle[51] method. This makes it easier to update the notifications by combining multiple notifications under a single expandable notification, as shown in Listing 6-33.

---

[50]http://developer.android.com/reference/android/app/Notification.
InboxStyle.html.
[51]http://developer.android.com/reference/android/app/Notification.
Builder.html#setStyle(android.app.Notification.Style).

Listing 6-33. Combining Notifications Under a Single Notification Using the Inbox Style

```
Notification.InboxStyle inboxStyle =
        new Notification.InboxStyle();
inboxStyle.addLine("Fw: Information you have requested");
inboxStyle.addLine("New books on sale at Apress.com");
inboxStyle.setSummaryText("+2 more");

notification = new Notification.Builder(this)
        .setContentTitle("You have 4 New Messages")
        .setContentText("onur.cinar@gmail.com")
        .setSmallIcon(R.drawable.ic_apress)
        .setContentIntent(pendingIntent)
        .setStyle(inboxStyle)
        .build();

notificationManager.notify(1, notification);
```

Canceling a Notification

If the notification is no longer needed, the application can use the cancel[52] method of the NotificationManager to cancel an existing notification by providing its unique notification identifier, as shown in Listing 6-34.

Listing 6-34. Canceling a Notification Using the Unique Notification ID

```
notificationManager.cancel(1);
```

The application can also cancel all of its notifications through the cancelAll[53] method of the NotificationManager class, as shown in Listing 6-35.

Listing 6-35. Canceling All Application Notifications

```
notificationManager.cancelAll();
```

---

[52]http://developer.android.com/reference/android/app/
NotificationManager.html#cancel(int).
[53]http://developer.android.com/reference/android/app/
NotificationManager.html#cancelAll().

Summary

This chapter provided a brief overview of the APIs that are employed by the Android framework to benefit from base window features, such as the action bar, toasts, dialogs, and notifications. The action bar is part of every Android application starting from API Level 11. It delivers a consistent way to provide identification about the application and a prominent place to list import application actions. Toasts and dialogs provide a way to launch a pop-up window to deliver notification to the user, and also to prompt the user for information while the application is still in the foreground. In a similar way, notifications allow applications to notify the user while the application is backgrounded. Once the notification gets posted for displaying in the notification area, the Android platform also propagates the notification to connected devices, such as smart watches. Proper use of these window features improves the user experience and provides a consistent way for users to interact with Android applications.

Chapter 7

Storing Data

The Android framework provides several options to store application data. There is no single best storage option, as the options depend on the application and the use cases. This chapter briefly goes through each of the storage options offered by the Android framework, such as simple files, shared preferences, and the relational databases. Later in this chapter, we will explore Android Backup Services as a mechanism to back up and restore application data to the cloud in order make it persist between device upgrades and device resets.

Simple Files

As with all platforms, the easiest way to persist data on the Android platform is by saving the data in files on the device's storage. You can achieve this with file I/O APIs (input/output application programming interfaces) provided by the Java programming language. The Android platform provides two storage types, *internal storage* (nonremovable) and *external storage* (such as a removable SD card).

Using Internal Storage

By default, the data saved on the internal storage is private to the application itself. Once the application gets uninstalled, Android removes these files along the application. A new file can be created on the internal storage by using the Context.openFileOutput[1] method through the current context, such as the current activity. The method will return a java.io.OutputStream for writing to the file, as shown in Listing 7-1.

---

[1]http://developer.android.com/reference/android/content/Context.html#openFileOutput(java.lang.String,int).

Listing 7-1. Opening a File on Internal Storage for Appending

```
try {
    FileOutputStream output =
            openFileOutput("file.dat", MODE_APPEND);
    try {
        // write to output stream
    } finally {
        output.close();
    }
} catch (IOException e) {
    e.printStackTrace();
}
```

The getFileOutput method takes a *file name* to open or create for output and a *file mode* to use. The file mode is a list of flags that can be specified to control how the file should be opened by the API. The file mode can be a combination of the following:

- MODE_PRIVATE is the default file mode if no mode gets specified. The created file can only be accessed by the calling application.

- MODE_APPEND instructs Android to open the file in append mode, instead of erasing it, if the file already exists.

> **Caution**   The Android platform also supported other modes such as MODE_WORLD_READABLE and MODE_WORLD_WRITABLE, but they are now deprecated due to security concerns. To share data with other applications on the device, you should use more formal mechanisms, such as *Content Providers*, instead.

You can then open the same file for reading using the Context. openFileInput[2] method and by providing the file name, as shown in Listing 7-2.

Listing 7-2. Opening a File on Internal Storage for Reading

```
File input = openFileInput("file.dat");
```

---

[2]http://developer.android.com/reference/android/content/Context.html# openFileInput(java.lang.String).

Using External Storage

For larger files, I recommend using external storage as internal storage is a scarce resource on most Android devices. The files saved on external storage are readable and writable by anyone when the user enables USB mass storage to mount external storage to an attached computer for transferring files.

> **Caution**   When external storage gets mounted as USB mass storage on a computer, it will become unavailable to the applications that are running on the device.

Getting Access to External Storage

Using external storage for reading and writing does require a certain permission. The application must request this permission through the manifest file, as shown in Listing 7-3, during the install time.

Listing 7-3. Requesting Write Access to External Storage in the Manifest File

```
<uses-permission android:name=
    "android.permission.WRITE_EXTERNAL_STORAGE" />
```

Access to external storage is controlled by two permissions:

- READ_EXTERNAL_STORAGE for reading from external storage.

- WRITE_EXTERNAL_STORAGE for both reading and writing to external storage.

Checking If External Storage Is Available

As mentioned earlier in this section, external storage is removable, and it may not be always available for the applications. Before trying to use external storage, the application should always check its availability by using the `Environment.getExternalStorageState`[3] method. This method can return any of the following constant strings to indicate the current state of the external storage:

- `MEDIA_UNKNOWN`: Unknown storage state. External storage is not usable.

- `MEDIA_REMOVED`: External storage is not currently attached to the device.

- `MEDIA_UNMOUNTED`: External storage is attached to the device, but the file system is not mounted yet. External storage cannot be used at this state.

- `MEDIA_CHECKING`: External storage is attached but going through a disk check.

- `MEDIA_NOFS`: External storage is attached, but it does not have a known file system on it. It cannot be used at this state.

- `MEDIA_MOUNTED`: External storage is attached and mounted. It can be used by the applications.

- `MEDIA_READ_ONLY`: External storage is attached and mounted in read-only mode. Applications can read the files on the external storage, but they cannot write to them.

- `MEDIA_SHARED`: External storage is currently shared through the USB mass storage with an attached computer.

- `MEDIA_BAD_REMOVAL`: External storage was previously removed improperly. It will require checking.

- `MEDIA_UNMOUNTABLE`: External storage is attached to the device but the file system cannot be mounted. This may indicate that the media is corrupted.

The `getExternalStorageState` method can be used as shown in Listing 7-4 to check the availability of external storage before trying to access to it.

---

[3]http://developer.android.com/reference/android/os/Environment.html#get ExternalStorageState().

Listing 7-4. Checking the External Storage State Before Reading or Writing to It

```
String state = Environment.getExternalStorageState();

boolean canWrite = Environment.MEDIA_MOUNTED.equals(state);
if (canWrite) {
    // write to external storage
}

boolean canRead =
            Environment.MEDIA_MOUNTED_READ_ONLY.equals(state)
        || Environment.MEDIA_MOUNTED.equals(state);

if (canRead) {
    // read from external stroage
}
```

Getting the Path to External Storage

You can obtain the path to the external storage top-level directory through the `Enviroment.getExternalStorageDirectory`[4] method, as shown in Listing 7-5.

Listing 7-5. Getting the External Storage Directory

```
File externalStorage =
        Environment.getExternalStorageDirectory();
```

It is recommended that the applications should not use this top-level directory in order to prevent polluting the user's external storage. Depending on different file types and use cases, Android provides APIs to obtain the proper directory.

Storing Application Internal Files on External Storage

You can use the `Context.getExternalFilesDir`[5] method of the current context to obtain the external storage directory that the application should use to store its internal files. As with internal storage, the files that are stored in this directory will be removed when the application gets uninstalled. Android does not enforce any security on that directory, as any application with access to the external storage can read and manipulate these files.

---

[4]http://developer.android.com/reference/android/os/Environment.html#get ExternalStorageDirectory().
[5]http://developer.android.com/reference/android/content/Context.html# getExternalFilesDir(java.lang.String).

The getExternalFilesDir[6] method also takes a type parameter to return a special subdirectory for the given file type as shown in Listing 7-6. If this parameter is set to null, the top-level directory will be returned. The following types are supported as constants on the android.os.Environment class:

- DIRECTORY_ALARMS: Directory to store alarm sound files.

- DIRECTORY_DCIM: Traditional directory for pictures and video when mounting the device as a camera.

- DIRECTORY_DOCUMENTS: Directory to store document files.

- DIRECTORY_DOWNLOADS: Directory to store files that are downloaded.

- DIRECTORY_MOVIES: Directory to store videos.

- DIRECTORY_MUSIC: Directory to store audio and music files.

- DIRECTORY_NOTIFICATIONS: Directory to store notification sound files.

- DIRECTORY_PICTURES: Directory to store pictures.

- DIRECTORY_PODCASTS: Directory to store podcasts.

- DIRECTORY_RINGTONES: Directory to store ringtones.

Listing 7-6. Getting the External Application Internal Pictures Directory

```
File externalPictures =
        getExternalFilesDir(Environment.DIRECTORY_PICTURES);
```

Storing Public Files on External Storage

An application can also store public files on external storage. As it is recommended not to store them on the top-level directory, the application should use the Environment.getExternalStoragePublicDirectory[7] method with the directory type based on the file to store, as shown in Listing 7-7. The directory types are the same ones that were listed previously.

---

[6]http://developer.android.com/reference/android/content/Context.html# getExternalFilesDir(java.lang.String).
[7]http://developer.android.com/reference/android/os/Environment.html# get ExternalStoragePublicDirectory(java.lang.String).

Listing 7-7. Getting the External Public Music Storage Directory

```
File publicMusic =
        Environment.getExternalStoragePublicDirectory(
                Environment.DIRECTORY_MUSIC);
```

Caching Data Using Storage

Cache is a temporary storage to provide faster access to data that can otherwise be retrieved through another mechanism. For example, a big data file that is downloaded from the network could be placed into the cache directory in order to make it faster for the application to reach it the next time. If the device runs low on storage, Android deletes these files to free space. At that stage, the file simply needs to be retrieved again by the application.

In order to simply cache data, the following two methods can be used:

- ▓ `Context.getCacheDir`:[8] to get the application's cache directory on the internal storage.

- ▓ `Context.getExternalCacheDir`:[9] to get the application's cache directory on the external storage.

As the cache directory is application specific, it gets deleted when the application gets uninstalled.

Structuring Data Through JSON

Using plain files to store data has challenges as managing the records on a file can easily become a cumbersome task based on the complexity of the data itself. The JavaScript Object Notation (JSON) format is a human-readable text format to store data as attribute-value pairs. The Android framework provides APIs to read and write data in JSON format. Applications can rely on JSON format to persist data easily on both internal and external storage.

---

[8]http://developer.android.com/reference/android/content/Context.html# getCacheDir().

[9]http://developer.android.com/reference/android/content/Context.html# getExternalCacheDir().

Writing Data Using JSON Format

The android.util.JsonWriter[10] class can be used to write a JSON stream on an output stream, as shown in Listing 7-8.

Listing 7-8. Writing Data to Internal Storage in JSON Format

```
try {
    JsonWriter jsonWriter = new JsonWriter(
            new OutputStreamWriter(
                    openFileOutput(
                            "data.json", MODE_PRIVATE)));
    try {
        // Use indention to make file human-readable
        jsonWriter.setIndent("    ");

        jsonWriter.beginObject();

        jsonWriter.name("name");
        jsonWriter.value("Onur Cinar");

        jsonWriter.name("email");
        jsonWriter.value("onur.cinar@gmail.com");

        jsonWriter.endObject();
    } finally {
        jsonWriter.close();
    }
} catch (IOException e) {
    e.printStackTrace();
}
```

Listing 7-9 also shows the JSON file that is generated.

Listing 7-9. The JSON Formatted Data File on Internal Storage

```
{
    "name": "Onur Cinar",
    "email": "onur.cinar@gmail.com"
}
```

---

[10]http://developer.android.com/reference/android/util/JsonWriter.html.

Reading Data Using JSON Format

The data file that is created in the previous example can easily be read by using the android.util.JsonReader[11] class as shown in Listing 7-10.

Listing 7-10. Reading Data from Internal Storage in JSON Format

```
try {
    JsonReader jsonReader = new JsonReader(
            new InputStreamReader(
                    openFileInput("data.json")));
    try {
        jsonReader.beginObject();

        while (jsonReader.hasNext()) {
            String name = jsonReader.nextName();

            if ("name".equals(name)) {
                String firstName = jsonReader.nextString();
            } else if ("email".equals(name)) {
                String email = jsonReader.nextString();
            } else {
                // Unknown attribute skip value
                jsonReader.skipValue();
            }
        }

        jsonReader.endObject();
    } finally {
        jsonReader.close();
    }
} catch (IOException e) {
    e.printStackTrace();
}
```

> **Tip**   The JSON library that is provided as part of the Android framework is a very low-level library requiring decent amount of code to operate. Gson (https://code.google.com/p/google-gson/) is a more advanced and easier to use JSON library alternative.

---

[11]http://developer.android.com/reference/android/util/JsonReader.html.

Shared Preferences

Android provides a comprehensive framework for easily persisting data as key-value pairs through the android.content.SharedPreferences[12] class. For any particular set of preferences, Android only keeps a single instance of this class in order to keep the integrity of the data. Shared preferences are stored within internal storage, and they are removed when the application gets uninstalled.

Opening Shared Preferences

Although fundamentally they are the same, the Android framework provides two types of shared preferences: the activity shared preferences and the generic shared preferences.

Opening the Activity Shared Preferences

The Acitivty.getPreferences[13] method can be used from an activity context to get a shared preference that is private to the current activity, as shown in Listing 7-11.

Listing 7-11. Getting the Activity Private Shared Preferences

```
SharedPreferences sharedPreferences =
        getPreferences(MODE_PRIVATE);
```

Opening the Default Shared Preferences

The PreferenceManager.getDefaultSharedPreferences method can be used to obtain the shared preferences instance for the context, as shown in Listing 7-12. I recommend using the default shared preferences in order to use the *Preference Screen*, discussed later in this section.

Listing 7-12. Getting the Default Shared Preferences for the Application

```
SharedPreferences sharedPreferences =
        PreferenceManager.getDefaultSharedPreferences(this);
```

---

[12]http://developer.android.com/reference/android/content/Shared Preferences.html.
[13]http://developer.android.com/reference/android/app/Activity.html#get Preferences(int).

Opening the Generic Shared Preferences

Generic shared preferences files can also be created and used by employing the Context.getSharedPreferences[14] method and by providing a file name, as shown in Listing 7-13. The getSharedPreferences method also takes a file permission mode similar to the Context.openOutputFile method.

Listing 7-13. Opening a Shared Preferences File

```
SharedPreferences sharedPreferences =
        getShredPreferences("application", MODE_PRIVATE);
```

Adding and Editing Shared Preferences

New shared preferences can be added, and the existing ones can be edited by getting a SharedPreferences.Editor[15] class instance from the shared preferences object by calling the SharedPreferences.edit[16] method. The Editor class provides various methods to store preference values in all fundamental data types. The modifications can then be saved to the shared preferences by calling the Editor.commit[17] method as shown in Listing 7-14.

Listing 7-14. Editing the Shared Preferences

```
SharedPreferences.Editor editor = sharedPreferences.edit();

editor.putString("name", "Onur Cinar");
editor.putBoolean("registered", true);

editor.commit();
```

Reading the Shared Preferences

The key-value pairs in the shared preferences can be ready anytime by using the getter methods on the SharedPreferences class, as shown in Listing 7-15.

---

[14]http://developer.android.com/reference/android/content/ContextWrapper
.html#getSharedPreferences(java.lang.String,int).
[15]http://developer.android.com/reference/android/content/Shared
Preferences.Editor.html.
[16]http://developer.android.com/reference/android/content/Shared
Preferences.html#edit().
[17]http://developer.android.com/reference/android/content/Shared
Preferences.Editor.html#commit().

Listing 7-15. Reading from the Shared Preferences

```
String name =
        sharedPreferences.getString("name", null);

boolean registered =
        sharedPreferences.getBoolean("registered", false);
```

The last parameter of the getter method is the default value that should be returned if you do not find the requested preferences key in the shared preferences. The application can also check if a preference exists by using the SharedPreferences.contains[18] method.

Listening for Shared Preferences Changes

Application components can also register to be notified on shared preferences changes using the SharedPreferences.registerOnSharedPreferenceChangeListener[19] method, as shown in Listing 7-16.

Listing 7-16. Registering for Shared Preferences Change Events

```
SharedPreferences.OnSharedPreferenceChangeListener listener =
    new SharedPreferences.OnSharedPreferenceChangeListener() {
    @Override
    public void onSharedPreferenceChanged(
            SharedPreferences sharedPreferences, String key) {
        if (!sharedPreferences.contains(key)) {
            // shared preference is removed
        } else {
            // get the new value
        }
    }
};

sharedPreferences.registerOnSharedPreferenceChangeListener(
        listener);
```

---

[18]http://developer.android.com/reference/android/content/Shared Preferences.html#contains(java.lang.String).
[19]http://developer.android.com/reference/android/content/Shared Preferences.html#registerOnSharedPreferenceChangeListener (android.content.SharedPreferences.OnSharedPreferenceChangeListener).

The application component can unregister from receiving these notifications anytime by calling the SharedPreferences. unregisterOnSharedPreferenceChangeListener method, as shown in Listing 7-17.

Listing 7-17. Unregistering to Receive Shared Preferences Change Events

```
sharedPreferences.unregisterOnSharedPreferenceChangeListener(
        listener);
```

Preferences Screen

The Android framework also provides a fragment class, android. preference.PreferenceFragment,[20] which can automatically generate a user interface (UI) screen to let the user manipulate the default shared preferences through the UI components. This makes it easier to quickly create settings screens in a consistent manner.

Configuring the Preferences Screen

The PreferenceFragment gets configured in an XML resource file through the <PreferenceScreen>[21] XML tag. This configuration file defines which preferences should be edited through UI, and through which UI components, as shown in Listing 7-18.

Listing 7-18. Preferences Screen Configuration Resource

```
<PreferenceScreen
    xmlns:android="http://schemas.android.com/apk/res/android">

    <PreferenceCategory android:title=
        "@string/preferences_category_title_basic_preferences">

    <EditTextPreference
        android:key="name"
        android:title="@string/preferences_title_name"
        android:summary="@string/preferences_summary_name" />
    </PreferenceCategory>
</PreferenceScreen>
```

---

[20]http://developer.android.com/reference/android/preference/Preference Fragment.html.
[21]http://developer.android.com/reference/android/preference/Preference Screen.html.

The configuration specifies that the shared preference named "name" should be available for modifications through UI, and it will be modified through the text editor UI component. The following editors are also supported:

- ▦ `<CheckBoxPreference>`:[22] Provides a check box to edit a Boolean preference.

- ▦ `<ListPreference>`:[23] Provides a dialog with list of options to edit a preference.

- ▦ `<EditTextPreference>`:[24] Provides a dialog with a text input to edit a preference.

Displaying the Preference Screen

The preference screen can be displayed by inheriting a new fragment class from the android.preference.PreferenceFragment and setting the preference configuration to use, as shown in Listing 7-19.

Listing 7-19. Inheriting a New Fragment Class from the Preference Fragment

```
public class BasicPreferenceFragment extends PreferenceFragment {
    @Override
    public void onCreate(Bundle savedInstanceState) {
        super.onCreate(savedInstanceState);

        addPreferencesFromResource(R.xml.basic_preferences);
    }
}
```

The new fragment can then be displayed as an ordinary fragment. The preferences screen looks as shown in Figure 7-1.

---

[22]http://developer.android.com/reference/android/preference/CheckBox Preference.html.
[23]http://developer.android.com/reference/android/preference/List Preference.html.
[24]http://developer.android.com/reference/android/preference/EditText Preference.html.

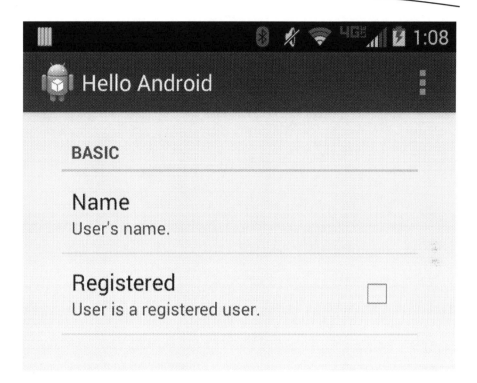

Figure 7-1. *Preferences screen*

SQLite Relational Database

The Android framework comes with support for storing the data in a relational database. Android relies on the well-known SQLite embedded database to power this feature. The Android framework provides wrapper classes and helper methods to interact with the native SQLite library functions from the application space.

Creating and Opening the Database

A new SQLite database can be created simply by extending the android.database.sqlite.SQLiteOpenHelper[25] abstract class and providing the implementations for both the onCreate and the onUpgrade methods. As shown in Listing 7-20, the constructor for SQLiteOpenHelper expects the *database name* and the *database version number*, besides the current context and an optional cursor factory.

---

[25]http://developer.android.com/reference/android/database/sqlite/SQLite OpenHelper.html.

Listing 7-20. Opening an SQLite Database

```java
public class DataStore extends SQLiteOpenHelper {
    /** Database name. */
    private static final String DB_NAME = "datastore";

    /** Database version. */
    private static final int DB_VERSION = 2;

    public DataStore(Context context) {
        super(context, DB_NAME, null, DB_VERSION);
    }

    @Override
    public void onCreate(SQLiteDatabase sqLiteDatabase) {

    }

    @Override
    public void onUpgrade(SQLiteDatabase sqLiteDatabase,
                          int oldVersion, int newVersion) {

    }
}
```

> **Caution** Database operations require disk I/O and may take a longer time to complete. An application should not invoke any database operation within the main thread (UI thread) in order to prevent possible UI freezes and ANR (application not responding) dialog.

During runtime, if the database does not exist, the onCreate[26] method gets called to let the application prepare the database by creating the database tables. If the database exists but the database version number is lower than the one provided to the constructor, the onUpgrade[27] method gets called to allow the application to do the necessary steps to upgrade the database schema.

---

[26]http://developer.android.com/reference/android/database/sqlite/SQLite OpenHelper.html#onCreate(android.database.sqlite.SQLiteDatabase).
[27]http://developer.android.com/reference/android/database/sqlite/ SQLite OpenHelper.html#onUpgrade(android.database.sqlite.SQLiteDatabase, int,int).

> **Note**   In case of a downgrade, the onDowngrade method can be overridden to provide the steps to downgrade a database schema. By default, the SQLiteOpenHelper throws an exception if the database version is higher than the one provided to the constructor.

Creating Tables

You can create database tables in the onCreate method by issuing one or more CREATE TABLE[28] SQL queries, as shown in Listing 7-21. Android simply provides a wrapper around SQLite; all SQL commands and data types that are supported by SQLite can be used from the Java space.

Listing 7-21. Creating the Database Tables

```
@Override
public void onCreate(SQLiteDatabase sqLiteDatabase) {
    sqLiteDatabase.execSQL(
            "CREATE TABLE address_book ("
        + "name TEXT PRIMARY KEY"
        + ", email TEXT NOT NULL"
        + ")"
    );
}
```

The foregoing example code creates a table named address_book with two columns, name and email, both using TEXT data type. The PRIMARY KEY column constraint on the name column indicates that the name will be the unique identifier for the data rows, so that it cannot contain any duplicates.

Upgrading the Existing Database

During runtime, if an existing database is found with a lower database version number, the onUpgrade method gets called with both the new and old database version numbers. Depending on the version of the existing database, the application can issue a set of SQL queries to upgrade the database schema and the data to the newer version. As shown in Listing 7-22, the ALTER TABLE[29] SQL query can be used to manipulate the database tables.

---

[28]www.sqlite.org/lang_createtable.html.
[29]www.sqlite.org/lang_altertable.html.

Listing 7-22. Upgrading an Existing Database by Altering Database Tables

```
@Override
public void onUpgrade(SQLiteDatabase sqLiteDatabase,
                      int oldVersion, int newVersion) {
    if (oldVersion == 1) {
        sqLiteDatabase.execSQL(
                "ALTER TABLE address_book"
            + " ADD COLUMN email TEXT NOT NULL");
    }
}
```

Writing to the Database

In order to write to the database, you can obtain a writable database object using the getWritableDatabase[30] method of the class extending the SQLiteOpenHelper, as shown in Listing 7-23.

Listing 7-23. Getting a Writable Database Instance

```
SQLiteDatabase sqLiteDatabase =
        dataStore.getWritableDatabase();
```

Inserting Data into the Database

You can insert data rows into the writable table by using the INSERT[31] SQL query. The Android SQLite wrapper provides a helper method called SQLiteDatabase.insert[32] for this operation. The insert method takes the name of the table, an android.content.ContentValues bundle holding the data as key-value pairs, as shown in Listing 7-24.

> **Note** As mentioned earlier in this section, you are not limited only by the helper methods provided by the Android SQLite wrapper objects. You can issue any valid SQLite command through the execSQL method to make database manipulations, including adding new data to the database.

---

[30]http://developer.android.com/reference/android/database/sqlite/SQLite OpenHelper.html#getWritableDatabase().
[31]www.sqlite.org/lang_insert.html.
[32]http://developer.android.com/reference/android/database/sqlite/ SQLite Database.html#insert(java.lang.String,java.lang.String,android. content.ContentValues).

Listing 7-24. Inserting a New Data Row in the Database

```
public void add(String name, String email) {
    ContentValues contentValues = new ContentValues();
    contentValues.put("name", name);
    contentValues.put("email", email);

    SQLiteDatabase sqLiteDatabase = getWritableDatabase();
    sqLiteDatabase.insert("address_book", null, contentValues);
}
```

> **Tip**   Persisting data from an object structure may become cumbersome work. Although the Android framework does not directly provide them, there are various Object Relational Mapping libraries supporting the Android platform, such as the OrmLite (http://ormlite.com/sqlite_java_android_orm.shtml).

Updating Existing Data in the Database

Data that is already in the database can be manipulated through the UPDATE[33] SQL query. The SQLiteDatabase.update[34] helper method is provided for this operation. As shown in Listing 7-25, the method takes the table name, values to update, and an SQL WHERE[35] clause indicating which data rows should be updated.

> **Tip**   Value substitution is supported in the SQL WHERE clause by using the question mark (?) as a placeholder for values. These placeholders get replaced with the values provided in the next parameter as a string array.

---

[33]www.sqlite.org/lang_update.html.
[34]http://developer.android.com/reference/android/database/sqlite/SQLite Database.html#update(java.lang.String,android.content.ContentValues, java.lang.String,java.lang.String[]).
[35]www.sqlite.org/lang_select.html#whereclause.

Listing 7-25. Updating the Existing Data in the Database

```
public void edit(String name, String email) {
    ContentValues contentValues = new ContentValues();
    contentValues.put("email", email);

    SQLiteDatabase sqLiteDatabase = getWritableDatabase();
    sqLiteDatabase.update("address_book", contentValues,
            "name=?", new String[] { name });
}
```

In the foregoing example code, the value of the email column on the address_book table gets updated only for the data rows with the name column matching the provided name.

Reading from the Database

In order to read data from the database, you can obtain a read-only database instance by calling the getReadableDatabase[36] of the class extending the SQLiteOpenHelper class, as shown in Listing 7-26.

Listing 7-26. Getting a Readable Database Instance

```
SQLiteDatabase sqLiteDatabase =
        dataStore.getReadableDatabase();
```

Reading Data Rows from the Database

The SQLiteDatabase.query[37] method enables you to run SQLite database queries that can return one or more rows of data. The data is returned by the query method as an android.database.Cursor[38] instance. As shown in Listing 7-27, the application code then can iterate through this cursor to extract the returned data set one row each time.

---

[36]http://developer.android.com/reference/android/database/sqlite/SQLite OpenHelper.html#getReadableDatabase().
[37]http://developer.android.com/reference/android/database/sqlite/SQLite Database.html#query(java.lang.String,java.lang.String[],java.lang. String,java.lang.String[],java.lang.String,java.lang.String,java.lang. String,java.lang.String).
[38]http://developer.android.com/reference/android/database/Cursor.html.

Listing 7-27. Reading Data Rows from the Database

```
public List<String> getAllEmails() {
    SQLiteDatabase sqLiteDatabase = getReadableDatabase();

    Cursor cursor = sqLiteDatabase.query(
            "address_book", new String[]{"email"},
            null, null, null, null,
            "ORDER BY email");

    LinkedList<String> emails = new LinkedList<String>();
    if (cursor.moveToFirst()) {
        do {
            emails.add(cursor.getString(0));
        } while(cursor.moveToNext());
    }

    return emails;
}
```

The query method takes the following parameters:

- ▨ table: Table name.

- ▨ columns: String array consisting of column names to retrieve.

- ▨ selection: An optional SQL WHERE clause to select which data rows to return, passing null returns all data rows.

- ▨ selectionArgs: An optional list of parameter (?'s) values to be substituted in selection.

- ▨ groupBy: Optional filter on how the rows should be grouped using the GROUP BY[39] clause.

- ▨ having: Optional filter on which row groups to be returned using the HAVING clause.

- ▨ orderBy: Optional filter on how the rows should be ordered using the ORDER BY[40] clause.

- ▨ limit: Optional limit on maximum number of rows to return using the LIMIT[41] clause.

---

[39]www.sqlite.org/lang_select.html#resultset.
[40]www.sqlite.org/lang_select.html#orderby.
[41]www.sqlite.org/lang_select.html#limitoffset.

Deleting Data from the Database

Data in the database can be deleted by using the DELETE SQL query. The Android SQLite wrapper provides the SQLiteDatabase.delete[42] helper method for this operation. As shown in Listing 7-28, the delete method takes the table name and an SQL WHERE clause to filter the data rows to be deleted.

Listing 7-28. Deleting Data from the Database

```
public void delete(String name) {
    SQLiteDatabase sqLiteDatabase = getWritableDatabase();
    sqLiteDatabase.delete("address_book",
            "name=?", new String[] {name});
}
```

Deleting the Entire Database

You can also delete the entire database by calling the Context.deleteDatabase[43] method and providing the database name, as shown in Listing 7-29.

Listing 7-29. Deleting the Entire Database

```
public static void deleteDatabase(Context context) {
    context.deleteDatabase(DB_NAME);
}
```

Android Backup Service

Due to the speed of technological enhancement in the mobile field, the average lifespan of a mobile device is around two years. Mobile phone users upgrade their devices to a newer model almost every two years. Android helps to smooth this process by continuously backing up the list of the user's downloaded applications and system settings to the cloud. Once the user upgrades to a new mobile device, Android seamlessly restores the applications and system settings.

---

[42]http://developer.android.com/reference/android/database/sqlite/SQLite
Database.html#delete(java.lang.String,java.lang.String,java.lang.
String[]).
[43]http://developer.android.com/reference/android/content/Context.html#
deleteDatabase(java.lang.String).

Although this makes it possible for the applications to follow the user as the user upgrades to new mobile devices, the application data is not carried with this process by default. Application developers are expected to explicitly sign up for the *Android Backup Service*,[44] and to provide a custom implementation of android.app.backup.BackupAgent[45] in their application to interact with the Android Backup Service.

Signing Up for Android Backup Service

Applications that support data backup should register for the Android Backup Service through the signup page at https://developer.android.com/google/backup/signup.html. As shown in Figure 7.2, you must first accept the terms of service and provide the application package name.

☑ I have read and agree with the Android Backup Service Terms of Service

Application package name: com.apress.helloandroid

Register with Android Backup Service

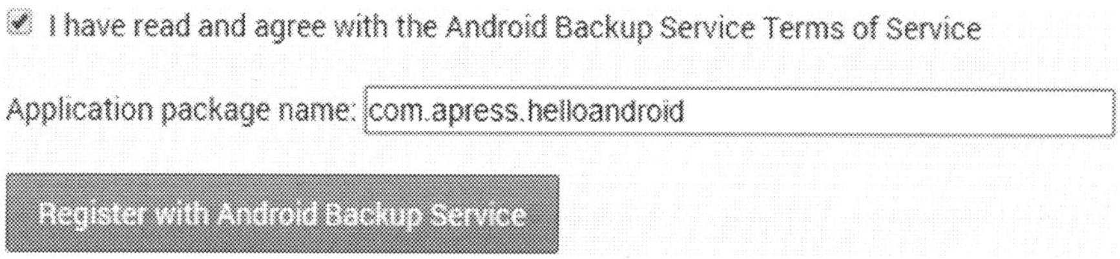

Figure 7-2. Android Backup Service signup page

Adding the Backup Service Key to the Manifest

Upon signing up for the Android Backup Service, you will receive a unique API key. This key needs to be incorporated into the application manifest file, AndroidManifest.xml, through a <meta-data> tag inside the <application> tag, as shown in Listing 7-30. You can simply copy and paste the <meta-data> line from the signup page into the application manifest file.

Listing 7-30. Adding the API Key into the Application Manifest

```
<application ...>
    <meta-data
        android:name="com.google.android.backup.api_key"
        android:value="AEd2zEfV3XzHSHqKxoIJAyYVZ6ZWnz4W_AmA" />
    ...
</application>
```

---

[44]http://developer.android.com/guide/topics/data/backup.html.
[45]http://developer.android.com/reference/android/app/backup/BackupAgent.html.

> **Note**   The Android Backup Service key that is provided here is simply a
> placeholder. You must register for a unique API key in order to experiment
> with the example code.

Providing the Backup Agent Implementation

The Android Backup Service does not automatically back up and restore
the application data directory. It requires the application to provide a backup
agent implementation to handle the application-specific backup and restore
operations. The easiest way to provide a backup agent is by extending
the android.app.backup.BackupAgentHelper[46] class. Upon extending the
BackupAgentHelper, simply override the onCreate method and specify the list
of things to be backed up by using the following helper classes:

- FileBackupHelper:[47] Manages backup and restore of a
  given list of files in the application's data directory.

- SharedPreferenceBackupHelper:[48] Manages backup and
  restore of shared preferences files.

> **Note**   To handle other data types that are not covered by the backup
> agent helper classes, you should extend the BackupAgent class and
> provide implementation for the backup and restore operations.

Each of these backup agent helpers can handle more than one entity, as
shown in Listing 7-31.

Listing 7-31. BackupAgentHelper Implementation

```
package com.apress.helloandroid;

import android.app.backup.BackupAgentHelper;
import android.app.backup.FileBackupHelper;
import android.app.backup.SharedPreferencesBackupHelper;
```

---

[46]http://developer.android.com/reference/android/app/backup/BackupAgent
Helper.html.
[47]http://developer.android.com/reference/android/app/backup/FileBackup
Helper.html.
[48]http://developer.android.com/reference/android/app/backup/Shared
PreferencesBackupHelper.html.

```
public class CloudBackupAgent extends BackupAgentHelper {
    @Override
    public void onCreate() {
        super.onCreate();

        addHelper("preferences",
                new SharedPreferencesBackupHelper(this,
                        getPackageName() + "_preferences",
                        "user"));

        addHelper("files",
                new FileBackupHelper(this,
                        "records.db"));
    }
}
```

The example code uses the SharedPreferenceBackupHelper to manage
the backup and restore of two shared preferences, the default shared
preferences and a generic shared preference called user.

> **Note**   The name for the default shared preferences is
> <package_name>_preferences. This name can be used with the
> SharedPreferenceBackupHelper to manage the backup and
> restore for it.

The code then uses the FileBackupHelper to manage the backup and
restore of records.db file.

> **Caution**   Any access to a file that is declared to be backed up must
> be synchronized as both the application and the backup service can
> manipulate the file at the same time, which may cause data corruption.

Declaring the Backup Agent in the Manifest

The backup agent implementation should then be declared in the application manifest file for the Android Backup Service to discover it. This is achieved by using the `android:backupAgent`[49] attribute of the `<application>` XML tag, as shown in Listing 7-32.

Listing 7-32. Declaring the Backup Agent in the Application Manifest

```
<application
    android:backupAgent=".CloudBackupAgent"
    >
```

Requesting Backup

In order to make sure that all application data is properly backed up on any modification, the application can request the Android Backup Service to do a backup by calling the `BackupManager.dataChanged`[50] method. The backup request gets scheduled and later executed by calling the methods of application's backup agent implementation.

Testing the Backup Agent Implementation

The backup agent implementation can be validated through the `bmgr`[51] command line tool that is part of the Android operating system.

> **Note**   Open Backup & Reset through the settings application that is on the device to make sure that Backup my data and Automatic restore are both enabled.

---

[49]http://developer.android.com/guide/topics/manifest/application-element.html#agent.

[50]http://developer.android.com/reference/android/app/backup/Backup Manager.html#dataChanged().

[51]http://developer.android.com/tools/help/bmgr.html.

Follow these steps to validate the backup agent implementation:

- Using the ADB (Android Debug Bridge) shell, manually trigger a backup request:

  ```
  adb shell bmgr backup com.apress.helloandroid
  ```

- Force the Android Backup Manager to do the backup:

  ```
  adb shell bmgr run
  ```

- Uninstall your application to make sure that all local data is erased:

  ```
  adb uninstall com.apress.helloandroid
  ```

- Install your application again and through the code validate that the data is properly restored.

Summary

This chapter explored the different storage options that are provided by the Android framework. As explained in this chapter, using simple files for storing data is the most generic storage option, although it does require a substantial amount of coding to handle both serializing and deserializing the data as plain files. Shared preferences is an Android-specific storage option for data that can be stored as key-value pairs. This storage option is the suggested format to store preferences data. The Android framework provides UI components to enable application developers to quickly produce settings screens on top of shared preferences. Finally, we explore SQLite database, the most advanced solution as a storage option for relational data. Compared to the other two storage options, the SQLite database allows the application to specify the format in which the data should be stored using database schemas. Later the application can manipulate and retrieve data from the relational database by simply executing SQL queries. The lifespan of the data stored on the device is tied to the lifespan of the device and operating system lifespans. The application data is not automatically restored when the user does a device reset, or simply upgrades to a new device. We explore Android Backup Service in the final section as a cloud-based solution to back up and restore application data.

Sensors and Location

The Android platform provides built-in sensors for measuring location, motion, orientation, and the characteristics of the surrounding environment. These sensors enable the development of location and environment-aware applications on the Android platform. This chapter explores the various sensors and location devices supported by the Android platform and the Android framework application programming interfaces (APIs) provided in order to interact with these sensors and location devices.

Sensor

Through the provided *sensor* APIs, Android applications can monitor the device's sensors in order to provide a highly interactive and compelling user experience. For example, most game applications extensively use the device's sensors as a way to obtain the user's input in a natural way. This section explores the APIs provided by the Android framework in order to interact with these sensors.

Sensor Manager

The Android framework provides access to the device's sensors through the Sensor Service. The application can access the Sensor Service through the SensorManager[1] APIs. The SensorManager instance can be retrieved through the getSystemService method, as shown in Listing 8-1.

---

[1]http://developer.android.com/reference/android/hardware/SensorManager.html.

Listing 8-1. Getting the SensorManager Instance

```
SensorManager sensorManager = (SensorManager)
        getSystemService(Context.SENSOR_SERVICE);
```

Sensor Types

Android supports various kinds of sensors. Some of those sensors are actual hardware sensors, part of the device, and some others are software-based sensors making their measurements by relying on a combination of other sensors. The Sensor[2] class provides a set of constants for each of these sensor types.

- TYPE_ACCELEROMETER: Accelerometer sensor—measures the acceleration force in m/s.[2]

- TYPE_AMBIENT_TEMPERATURE: Ambient temperature sensor—measures the ambient room temperature in Celsius.

- TYPE_GAME_ROTATION_VECTOR: Uncalibrated rotation vector sensor.

- TYPE_GEOMAGNETIC_ROTATION_VECTOR: Geomagnetic rotation vector sensor.

- TYPE_GRAVITY: Gravity sensor.

- TYPE_GYROSCOPE: Gyroscope sensor.

- TYPE_GYROSCOPE_UNCALIBRATED: Uncalibrated gyroscope sensor.

- TYPE_HEART_RATE: Heart rate sensor.

- TYPE_LIGHT: Light sensor.

- TYPE_LINEAR_ACCELERATION: Linear acceleration sensor.

- TYPE_MAGNETIC_FIELD: Magnetic field sensor.

- TYPE_MAGNETIC_FIELD_UNCALIBRATED: Uncalibrated magnetic field sensor.

- TYPE_PRESSURE: Pressure sensor.

- TYPE_PROXIMITY: Proximity sensor.

- TYPE_RELATIVE_HUMIDITY: Relative humidity sensor.

---

[2]http://developer.android.com/reference/android/hardware/Sensor.html.

▓ TYPE_ROTATION_VECTOR: Rotation vector sensor.

▓ TYPE_SIGNIFICANT_MOTION: Significant motion trigger sensor.

▓ TYPE_STEP_DETECTOR: Step detector sensor.

Getting the Default Sensor for a Given Type

Using the sensor-type constants provided in the previous list, the getDefaultSensor[3] method of SensorManager can be used to retrieve the default sensor for the given type, as shown in Listing 8-2.

> **Caution**   Although most sensors do not require a special permission, the newly introduced *body sensors*, such as the *heart rate sensor*, require the calling application to have the android.permission.BODY_SENSORS permission.

Listing 8-2. Getting the Default Sensor for a Given Sensor Type

```
Sensor sensor = sensorManager.getDefaultSensor(
        Sensor.TYPE_ACCELEROMETER);
if (sensor == null) {
    // Unable to get the sensor
} else {
    // Sensor can be used
}
```

Getting the List of All Sensors for a Given Type

The getDefaultSensor method only returns the default sensor for a given type. If the device is equipped with more than one sensor for any given sensor type, the application use getSensorList[4] method instead. The getSensorList method takes a sensor type and returns a list of sensors matching the given type. The application can go through the returned list and choose a sensor based on its characteristics, such as the sensor's resolution, as shown in Listing 8-3.

---

[3]http://developer.android.com/reference/android/hardware/SensorManager.html#getDefaultSensor(int).

[4]http://developer.android.com/reference/android/hardware/SensorManager.html#getSensorList(int).

Listing 8-3. Choosing a Sensor Based on Its Resolution

```
List<Sensor> sensors = sensorManager.getSensorList(
        Sensor.TYPE_ACCELEROMETER);

Sensor choosen = null;

if (sensors != null) {
    for (Sensor sensor : sensors) {
        if (choosen == null
        ||  choosen.getResolution() > sensor.getResolution()) {
            choosen = sensor;
        }
    }
}
```

Receiving Sensor Events

Once the sensor is obtained, the application can start listening for sensor events. Each sensor may report events in a different way. Before starting to listen for the sensor, the application should first check the sensor's reporting mode and choose the appropriate listening strategy.

Getting the Sensor's Reporting Mode

Each sensor can have only one reporting mode. The sensor's reporting mode can be retrieved through the getReportingMode method, as shown in Listing 8-4.

Listing 8-4. Getting the Sensor's Reporting Mode

```
int reportingMode = sensor.getReportingMode();
```

The Sensor class provides constants for each of the following supported reporting modes:

- ▓ REPORTING_MODE_CONTINUOUS: Events are reported at a constant rate which is set by the application.

- ▓ REPORTING_MODE_ON_CHANGE: Events are reported only when the measurement changes.

- ▓ REPORTING_MODE_ONE_SHOT: Events are reported in one-shot mode. Upon detection of an event, the sensor deactivates itself.

- ▓ REPORTING_MODE_SPECIAL_TRIGGER: Events are reported as described in the description of the sensor.

Receiving Sensor Events in Continuous and On-Change Modes

In both continuous reporting mode and on-change reporting mode, the application can simply register to receive the sensor events as they become available. The sensor events are delivered to the calling applications through a set of callback function calls.

Sensor Event Listener

The SensorEventListener[5] interface declares the callback functions. In order to receive sensor events, the application should provide an implementation of this interface, as shown in Listing 8-5.

Listing 8-5. Sensor Event Listener Implementation

```
public class SensorActivity extends Activity
        implements SensorEventListener {

    @Override
    public void onSensorChanged(SensorEvent sensorEvent) {
        // Sensor has new measurement
    }

    @Override
    public void onAccuracyChanged(Sensor sensor, int i) {
        // Sensor's accuracy has changed
    }
}
```

The SensorEventListener interface contains the following two callback functions:

- onAccuracyChanged: Called when the accuracy of sensor has changed.

- onSensorChanged: Called when sensor has new measurement values.

---

[5]http://developer.android.com/reference/android/hardware/ SensorEventListener.html.

Registering for Sensor Events

The application can then register itself to receive the sensor events through the registerListener[6] method of SensorManager. The registerListener method takes the SensorEventListener instance, the sensor instance, and the rate that the application expects to receive sensor events, as shown in Listing 8-6.

Listing 8-6. Registering to Receive Sensor Events

```
sensorManager.registerListener(this,
      sensor,
      SensorManager.SENSOR_DELAY_NORMAL);
```

The rate parameter is only a hint to the system, and it does not guarantee the delivery of sensor events at the given rate. Starting from API Level 9 onward, the rate can be provided in milliseconds. For the application developer's convenience, the Android framework also provides the following rate constants:

- ▓ SENSOR_DELAY_NORMAL: Default rate.
- ▓ SENSOR_DELAY_UI: Rate suitable for display purposes.
- ▓ SENSOR_DELAY_GAME: Rate suitable for games.
- ▓ SENSOR_DELAY_FASTEST: Fastest rate.

Unregistering from Sensor Events

When the application no longer needs to listen for sensor events, it can unregister itself using the unregisterListener method of SensorManager. Keeping the sensors active at all times will have significant battery-draining impact. As a best practice, the application should unregister in the onPause method before the application goes into the background, and register again in the onResume method when the application gets brought back to the foreground, as shown in Listing 8-7.

---

[6]http://developer.android.com/reference/android/hardware/SensorManager. html#registerListener(android.hardware.SensorEventListener,android. hardware.Sensor, int).

Listing 8-7. Unregistering from Sensor Events When Backgrounded

```
@Override
protected void onResume() {
    super.onResume();

    sensorManager.registerListener(this, sensor,
            SensorManager.SENSOR_DELAY_NORMAL);
}

@Override
protected void onPause() {
    super.onPause();

    sensorManager.unregisterListener(this);
}
```

Receiving One-Shot Trigger Sensor Events

Due to their purpose and their design, not all sensors support the provision of sensor readings at requested intervals. Such sensors usually get triggered by a certain event and then report a sensor reading to the application. The *significant motion sensor* is an example of such a sensor. It reports a sensor reading back to the application when a significant motion is detected. The trigger sensors automatically disable themselves after reporting the first one-shot event.

Trigger Event Listener

As only one event would get reported by the server, the Android framework provides a different listener, TriggerEventListener,[7] for listening to such events, as shown in Listing 8-8.

Listing 8-8. TriggerEventListener Implementation

```
public class OneShotListener extends TriggerEventListener {
    @Override
    public void onTrigger(TriggerEvent triggerEvent) {

    }
}
```

---

[7]http://developer.android.com/reference/android/hardware/
TriggerEventListener.html.

Requesting a One-Shot Sensor Event

As the trigger sensor does not run all the time, the application must explicitly request a measurement from the sensor as needed. This is achieved through the requestTriggerSensor[8] method of the SensorManager, as shown in Listing 8-9.

Listing 8-9. Requesting a Measurement from a Trigger Sensor

```
sensorManager.requestTriggerSensor(oneShotListener, sensor);
```

The requestTriggerSensor method takes the TriggerEventListener instance and the Sensor instance.

Canceling a Pending Measurement Request

As the trigger sensor simply waits for a certain condition to happen, the measurement result is not guaranteed to come immediately. The sensor runs until there is an event to report. As shown in Listing 8-10, if the application state changes and the measurement is no longer needed, the application can explicitly cancel the previous measurement request, through the cancelTriggerSensor method of SensorManager, in order to turn the sensor off.

Listing 8-10. Canceling a Pending Request from a Trigger Sensor

```
sensorManager.cancelTriggerSensor(oneShotListener, sensor);
```

Interpreting Sensor Events

As explained in the section "Sensor Event Listener," the sensor events are delivered to the application through the onSensorChanged callback method. The method takes a single parameter, the SensorEvent[9] object which is carrying the sensor event. The SensorEvent contains the following public members:

- ▓ accuracy: The accuracy of this sensor event.
- ▓ sensor: The source sensor of this event.

---

[8]http://developer.android.com/reference/android/hardware/SensorManager.h tml#requestTriggerSensor(android.hardware.TriggerEventListener,android. hardware.Sensor).

[9]http://developer.android.com/reference/android/hardware/SensorEvent. html.

▓   `timestamp`: The time in nanoseconds at which the event
     happened.

▓   `values`: Sensor-dependent measurement values.

Sensor Event Values Based on Sensor Type

The structure of the values array that is provided in the `SensorEvent` object
depends on the type of sensor that the event is originating from. Table 8-1
provides a list of sensor types and how their sensor event values
are structured.

Table 8-1. *Sensor Event Values Based on Sensor Type*

Sensor Type	Event Values	Description
TYPE_ACCELEROMETER	values[0]	Acceleration force along the x, y, z axes (m/s2).
	values[1]	
	values[2]	
TYPE_AMBIENT_TEMPERATURE	values[0]	Ambient temperature (°C).
TYPE_GAME_ROTATION_VECTOR	values[0]	Rotation vector component along x, y, z axes.
	values[1]	
	values[2]	
TYPE_GEOMAGNETIC_ ROTATION_VECTOR	values[0]	Rotation vector component along x, y, z axes.
	values[1]	
	values[2]	
TYPE_GRAVITY	values[0]	Force of gravity along the x, y, z axes (m/s2).
	values[1]	
	values[2]	
TYPE_GYROSCOPE	values[0]	Rate of rotation around the x, y, z axes (rad/s).
	values[1]	
	values[2]	

(continued)

Table 8-1. (*continued*)

Sensor Type	Event Values	Description
TYPE_GYROSCOPE_ UNCALIBRATED	values[0] values[1] values[2]	Rate of rotation without drift compensation around the x, y, z axes (rad/s).
TYPE_HEART_RATE	values[0]	Heart rate in beats per minute.
TYPE_LIGHT	values[0]	Illuminance (lx).
TYPE_LINEAR_ACCELERATION	values[0] values[1] values[2]	Acceleration force along x, y, z axes (m/s2) excluding gravity.
TYPE_MAGNETIC_FIELD	values[0] values[1] values[2]	Geomagnetic field strength along x, y, z axes (µT).
TYPE_MAGNETIC_FIELD_ UNCALIBRATED	values[0] values[1] values[2]	Geomagnetic field strength without hard iron calibration along x, y, z axes (µT).
TYPE_PRESSURE	values[0]	Ambient air pressure (hPa or mbar).
TYPE_PROXIMITY	values[0]	Distance from object (cm).
TYPE_RELATIVE_HUMIDITY	values[0]	Ambient relative humidity (%).
TYPE_ROTATION_VECTOR	values[0] values[1] values[2] values[3]	Rotation vector component along the x, y, z axes. Scalar component of the rotation vector.
TYPE_SIGNIFICANT_MOTION	N/A	N/A
TYPE_STEP_DETECTOR	values[0]	Number of steps taken by the user since the last reboot while the sensor was activated.

Location

Getting access to the user's current location allows certain applications to deliver relevant and better content to the user. For example, a restaurant search application can order the search results based on the user's distance to each restaurant to help the user to easily find the information needed. This section explores the location APIs provided by the Android framework.

Location Permissions

As tracking the user's current location raises privacy concerns, the location APIs are protected by a set of permissions. Only an application with the proper permissions is allowed to access the user's current location. The Android platform provides two location permissions.

- android.permission.ACCESS_COARSE_LOCATION: Allows the application to access the approximate location of the user. The location information is derived from network location sources such as cell towers and WiFi.

- android.permission.ACCESS_FINE_LOCATION: Allows the application to access the precise location of the user. The location information is based on a combination of GPS, network location sources, and WiFi.

Location Manager

The Android framework provides access to the device's sensors through the *location service*. The application can access the location service through the LocationManager[10] APIs. The LocationManager instance can be retrieved through the getSystemService method, as shown in Listing 8-11.

Listing 8-11. Getting the LocationManager Instance

```
LocationManager locationManager =
        (LocationManager) getSystemService(
                Context.LOCATION_SERVICE);
```

---

[10]http://developer.android.com/reference/android/location/
LocationManager.html.

Location Providers

The location service relies on the location providers to access the current location of the user. The LocationManager class provides constants for each of the supported location providers. The Android platform supports the following location providers:

- GPS_PROVIDER: It determines the location using the GPS satellites. Depending on environmental conditions, the provider may take a while to return a location fix. It requires ACCESS_FINE_LOCATION permission.

- NETWORK_PROVIDER: It determines the location using the availability of cell tower and WiFi access points.

- PASSIVE_PROVIDER: It determines the location without actually requesting a location fix. It relies on location requests that are requested by other applications. It requires ACCESS_FINE_LOCATION permission.

Checking If Location Provider Is Available

Not all location providers are available all the time. The Android platform allows the user to turn the location providers on and off through the settings application. Meanwhile, location providers may become unavailable if their information source, such as WiFi, are disabled. The LocationManager class provides the isProviderEnabled[11] method to allow applications to query the status of location providers, as shown in Listing 8-12.

Listing 8-12. Checking If the Location Provider Is Enabled

```
if (locationManager.isProviderEnabled(
        LocationManager.GPS_PROVIDER)) {
    // Use the GPS provider
} else {
    // Use an other provider
}
```

Listening for Location Provider State Changes

The Android platform allows the user to turn the location providers on and off through the settings application. The change in location providers gets broadcasted with the android.location.PROVIDERS_CHANGED action. As

---

[11]http://developer.android.com/reference/android/location/
LocationManager.html#isProviderEnabled(java.lang.String).

shown in Listing 8-13, applications can receive these broadcast messages to react according to location provider state changes, such as switching to the GPS location provider when it is enabled.

Listing 8-13. Registering for Provider-Changed Broadcast Messages

```
private final BroadcastReceiver providerChangedListener =
        new BroadcastReceiver() {
    @Override
    public void onReceive(Context context, Intent intent) {
        LocationManager locationManager =
                (LocationManager) context.getSystemService(
                        Context.LOCATION_SERVICE);

        if (locationManager.isProviderEnabled(
                LocationManager.GPS_PROVIDER)) {
            // Use the GPS provider
        } else {
            // Use an other provider
        }
    }
};

...

registerReceiver(providerChangedListener, new IntentFilter(
        LocationManager.PROVIDERS_CHANGED_ACTION));
```

Location Updates

The location provider allows an application to receive location updates in two ways. The application can either register to receive the location updates as the user's location changes or choose to register to receive a proximity alert only when the user enters the proximity of a given geographical location.

Continuous Location Updates

The application can register to receive continuous location updates by registering a location listener with the LocationManager.

Location Listener

Location updates get delivered to the application through a callback function that is declared in LocationListener[12] interface, as shown in Listing 8-14. The LocationListener interface, besides the location updates, also delivers updates regarding the status of the location provider in use, such as when the location provider gets enabled or disabled.

Listing 8-14. LocationListener Implementation

```
private final LocationListener locationListener =
        new LocationListener() {
    @Override
    public void onLocationChanged(Location location) {
        // Location update
    }

    @Override
    public void onStatusChanged(String provider, int status,
            Bundle extras) {
        // Provider status has changed
    }

    @Override
    public void onProviderEnabled(String provider) {
        // Provider enabled
    }

    @Override
    public void onProviderDisabled(String provider) {
        // Provider disabled
    }
};
```

Registering for Location Updates

The LocationListener instance can then be registered with the LocationManager using the requestLocationUpdates[13] method, as shown in Listing 8-15.

---

[12]http://developer.android.com/reference/android/location/
LocationListener.html.
[13]http://developer.android.com/reference/android/location/
LocationManager.html#requestLocationUpdates(java.lang.String, long,
float, android.location.LocationListener).

Listing 8-15. Registering for Location Updates

```
locationManager.requestLocationUpdates(
        LocationManager.GPS_PROVIDER,
        1000, // minimum 1 sec updates
        1, // minimum 1m changes
        locationListener);
```

The requestLocationUpdates method takes the name of the location provider to use, the minimum time interval between location updates, the minimum distance between location updates, and the LocationListener instance. The LocationManager provides various requstLocationUpdate methods for different use cases.

Unregistering from Location Updates

Similar to sensors, location devices also degrade the battery very rapidly. Applications are expected to unregister from location updates when they are not needed anymore. The LocationManager provides the removeUpdates method, as shown in Listing 8-16.

Listing 8-16. Unregistering from Location Updates

```
locationManager.removeUpdates(locationListener);
```

Requesting a Single Location Update

The application can also request a single location update using the requestSingleUpdate[14] method of LocationManager, as shown in Listing 8-17. The location device delivers a single location update and turns off.

Listing 8-17. Requesting a Single Location Update

```
locationManager.requestSingleUpdate(
        LocationManager.GPS_PROVIDER,
        locationListener,
        Looper.myLooper()
);
```

The LocationManager also supports registering for a single location update using a pending intent.

---

[14]http://developer.android.com/reference/android/location/
LocationManager.html#requestSingleUpdate(java.lang.String, android.
location.LocationListener, android.os.Looper).

Proximity Alerts

An application can register to be notified when the user enters the proximity of a given geographical location.

Adding a Proximity Alert

The addProximityAlert[15] method of LocationManager is used to register proximity alerts, as shown in Listing 8-18. The addProximityAlert method takes the latitude and longitude of the central point of the alert region, the radius of the central point of the alert in meters, an optional expiration time, and a pending intent to receive the alert.

Listing 8-18. Adding a Proximity Alert

```
locationManager.addProximityAlert(
        37.3688, // latitude
        -122.0363, // longitude
        100, // radius
        -1, // expiration
        PendingIntent.getActivity(this, 0, new Intent(this,
                LocationActivity.class), 0) // intent
);
```

Proximity alerts get delivered through the given pending intent. The intent contains a Boolean extra, KEY_PROXIMITY_ENTERING,[16] indicating whether the user is entering or exiting the proximity region.

Removing a Proximity Alert

Once it is no longer needed, the application can remove a proximity alert using the removeProximityAlert method of LocationManager, as shown in Listing 8-19.

Listing 8-19. Removing a Proximity Alert

```
locationManager.removeProximityAlert(pendingIntent);
```

---

[15]http://developer.android.com/reference/android/location/
LocationManager.html#addProximityAlert(double, double, float, long,
android.app.PendingIntent).
[16]http://developer.android.com/reference/android/location/
LocationManager.html#KEY_PROXIMITY_ENTERING.

Fast Location Fix Using Last Known Location

The time to receive the first location fix may take a long time, especially when using the GPS location provider. Until a more accurate location update is available, applications can simply use the getLastKnownLocation[17] method of LocationManager to retrieve the last known location, as shown in Listing 8-20.

Listing 8-20. Getting the Last Known Location

```
Location location = locationManager.getLastKnownLocation(
        LocationManager.NETWORK_PROVIDER);
```

Location Updates

Location updates are delivered to the application through Location[18] objects. The Location object contains the following information:

- Accuracy: The estimated accuracy of this location in meters.

- Altitude: The altitude, if available, in meters above World Geodetic System (WGS) 84 reference.

- Bearing: The bearing in degrees.

- Latitude and longitude: The coordinate in degrees.

- Provider: The name of the location provider.

- Time: Coordinated Universal Time (UTC) time of this location fix.

Summary

The Android platform provides environmental and location information to applications. The SensorManager API is used to interact with built-in sensors on the Android device. The sensor API provided by the Android framework is a generic API. Sensor events should be interpreted based on sensor type. Applications are expected to unregister receiving sensor events when needed, in order to conserve battery power on the device. Location support is provided through the LocationManager API. The Android platform supports

---

[17]http://developer.android.com/reference/android/location/
LocationManager.html#getLastKnownLocation(java.lang.String).
[18]http://developer.android.com/reference/android/location/Location.html.

various location providers, such as the GPS provider and the network provider. Due to privacy concerns, an application is expected to have certain permissions defined in order to access these location providers. The application can receive the user's current location in different ways based on the use case. The LocationManager also provides the last known location information to applications in order to compensate the latency of receiving the first location fix from a location provider.

Chapter 9

Media and Camera

Media support and access to a high-resolution camera are the most exciting features of the Android platform. Both of these features are very extensively used by Android applications. Dealing with media on a mobile device has its own unique challenges, and the Android framework provides a comprehensive application programming interface (API) for multimedia. This chapter provides a brief summary of those APIs and their usage.

Audio Manager

Android provides access to audio-related controls through the `android.media.AudioManager`[1] service. It can be accessed from the application code by requesting the system service instance for `Context.AUDIO_SERVICE` from the current context, as shown in Listing 9-1.

Listing 9-1. Getting the AudioManager Instance from the Current Context

```
AudioManager audioManager = (AudioManager)
        getSystemService(Context.AUDIO_SERVICE);
```

Audio Devices

Android devices are equipped with built-in audio input and output devices, such as the speakerphone and the microphone. Bluetooth headsets are also supported by such Android devices as external audio devices. The `AudioManager` class provides methods to check the current state of these devices, as well as enabling the application to toggle them.

---

[1]http://developer.android.com/reference/android/media/AudioManager.html.

Microphone

The microphone allows the Android device to receive audio input. When audio input is not needed, the microphone can be muted. The AudioManager class provides methods to check the current state of the microphone as well as enabling the application to mute and unmute the microphone.

Checking If the Microphone Is Muted

Using the isMicrophoneMute[2] method of the AudioManager class, the application can check if the microphone is muted, as shown in Listing 9-2.

Listing 9-2. Checking If Microphone Is Muted

```
if (audioManager.isMicrophoneMute()) {
    // stop streaming audio input
}
```

Muting and Unmuting the Microphone

Using the setMicrophoneMute method an application can mute and unmute the microphone, as shown in Listing 9-3, by passing a Boolean parameter.

Listing 9-3. Muting the Device's Microphone

```
audioManager.setMicrophoneMute(true);
```

Speakerphone

Android devices come with a speakerphone. The speakerphone allows the audio output to be heard from a short distance without the device being held to the face. The AudioManager provides methods to check the current state of the speakerphone, and also to route the audio output to the speakerphone as needed.

Checking If the Speakerphone Is On

Using the isSpeakerphoneOn[3] method of the AudioManager class, an application can check if the audio is played through the speakerphones, as shown in Listing 9-4.

---

[2]http://developer.android.com/reference/android/media/AudioManager. html#isMicrophoneMute().

[3]http://developer.android.com/reference/android/media/AudioManager. html#isSpeakerphoneOn().

Listing 9-4. Checking If the Speakerphone Is on

```
if (audioManager.isSpeakerphoneOn()) {
    // disable speakerphone button
}
```

Toggling the Speakerphone

The setSpeakerphoneOn method is also provided to allow an application to turn the speakerphone on or off, as shown in Listing 9-5.

Listing 9-5. Turning the Speakerphone on

```
audioManager.setSpeakerphoneOn(true);
```

Audio Streams

Android differentiates between audio streams based on their purpose, and it allows each of these stream groups to be controlled individually. This makes it possible for users to set different volume levels for different audio types, such as the alarm clock, the phone ring, and the music playback.

> **Caution**   As the Android platform cannot automatically determine the purpose of the audio played by applications, it is the application developer's responsibility to use the correct audio stream type depending on the purpose of the audio stream.

The AudioManager class provides constants for each of the following supported audio types:

- STREAM_ALARM: The audio stream for alarms.
- STREAM_DTMF: The audio stream for DTMF (dual-tone multi-frequency) tones.
- STREAM_MUSIC: The audio stream for music playback.
- STREAM_NOTIFICATION: The audio stream for notifications.
- STREAM_RING: The audio stream for phone rings.
- STREAM_SYSTEM: The audio stream for system sounds.
- STREAM_VOICE_CALL: The audio stream for phone calls.
- USE_DEFUALT_STREAM_TYPE: The default audio stream.

Adjusting the Audio Stream Volume

The volume of audio streams can be adjusted by the application through the methods provided by the AudioManager class.

Getting the Current Volume for the Audio Stream

Using the getStreamVolume[4] method of the AudioManager class, the application can query the current volume of a given audio stream, as shown in Listing 9-6.

Listing 9-6. Getting the Current Volume of the Music Audio Stream

```
int currentVolume = audioManager.getStreamVolume(
        AudioManager.STREAM_MUSIC);
```

> **Note**   The returned volume is simply an index value. Android allows each audio stream to have different volume ranges based on the device's capabilities. The volume percentage can be calculated by comparing this index value with the maximum volume index for the audio stream.

Getting the Maximum Volume for the Audio Stream

The getStreamMaxVolume[5] method of the AudioManager can be used to query the maximum volume index for a given stream, as shown in Listing 9-7.

Listing 9-7. Querying the Maximum Volume Index for Music Audio Stream

```
int maximumVolume = audioManager.getStreamMaxVolume(
        AudioManager.STREAM_MUSIC);
```

The application can then adjust the stream volume by providing a value between zero and the returned maximum volume index.

---

[4]http://developer.android.com/reference/android/media/AudioManager.html#getStreamVolume(int).
[5]http://developer.android.com/reference/android/media/AudioManager.html#getStreamMaxVolume(int).

Setting the Volume of an Audio Stream

The volume of an audio stream can be set using the setStreamVolume[6] method of the AudioManager class as shown in Listing 9-8. The same as other audio stream volume-related methods, the setStreamVolume method also takes a volume index to adjust the audio stream volume.

Listing 9-8. Setting the Volume of Music Audio Stream

```
audioManager.setStreamVolume(
        AudioManager.STREAM_MUSIC, 10,
        AudioManager.FLAG_SHOW_UI
            | AudioManager.FLAG_PLAY_SOUND);
```

As shown in Listing 9-8, the setStreamVolume method also takes a set of flags as the last parameter.

- FLAG_ALLOW_RINGER_MODES: Whether to include ringer modes when changing the volume—such as switching to silent or vibrate mode based on the volume index.

- FLAG_PLAY_SOUND: Whether to play a sound effect while switching the volume.

- FLAG_REMOVE_SOUND_AND_VIBRATE: Whether to suppress any sound or vibration that is queued or playing while changing the volume.

- FLAG_SHOW_UI: Whether to show a toast containing the current volume.

- FLAG_VIBRATE: Whether to vibrate if going into vibrate mode.

Muting the Audio Stream

Instead of lowering the audio stream volume to zero, the setStreamMute[7] method of the AudioManager class can be used to mute the audio stream, as shown in Listing 9-9.

Listing 9-9. Muting the Notification Audio Stream

```
audioManager.setStreamMute(
        AudioManager.STREAM_NOTIFICATION, true);
```

---

[6]http://developer.android.com/reference/android/media/AudioManager.
html#setStreamVolume(int, int, int).
[7]http://developer.android.com/reference/android/media/AudioManager.
html#setStreamMute(int, boolean).

The mute operation for a given stream is cumulative as multiple applications can request it simultaneously. AudioManager unmutes the stream only when the same number of unmute requests are received. Applications are expected to unmute a muted audio stream in their onPause method while going into background mode, and mute it again in onResume method when returning to the foreground.

> **Note**   The setStreamMute method is protected against process death. If the process crashes, the operating system automatically unmutes the stream.

Solo the Audio Stream

To play a single audio stream without any interference from other audio streams, the AudioManager class provides a method called setStreamSolo.[8] This method only allows the provided audio stream to play while it suppresses the other ones, as shown in Listing 9-10.

Listing 9-10. Soloing the Voice Audio Stream

```
audioManager.setStreamSolo(
        AudioManager.STREAM_VOICE_CALL, true);
```

The same as the operation to mute an audio stream, the solo operation for a given stream is cumulative and requires the same amount of un-solo requests in order to be disabled. Although the solo operation is protected against application process crashes, for a better user experience, we recommend that you un-solo the audio stream in onPause and solo the audio stream again in onResume when the application gets brought to the foreground.

Checking If Music Is Active

Using the isMusicActive[9] method of the AudioManager class, the application code checks if another application is playing music in the background, as shown in Listing 9-11.

---

[8]http://developer.android.com/reference/android/media/AudioManager.
html#setStreamSolo(int, boolean).
[9]http://developer.android.com/reference/android/media/AudioManager.
html#isMusicActive().

Listing 9-11. Checking If Another Application Is Playing Music

```
if (!audioManager.isMusicActive()) {
    // play sound effect
}
```

As in Listing 9-11, the application may decide not to play any sound effects while another application is playing music in the background.

Playing Audio

Audio playback has various use cases and also unique challenges for each of those use cases. The Android platform provides a set of audio APIs and constructs to address most frequent use cases, such as playing sound effects and playing music. This section briefly covers the most frequently used APIs.

MediaPlayer

The MediaPlayer[10] class is the core API provided by the Android framework for multimedia playback, both audio and video. This section only focuses on the audio aspect of the MediaPlayer.

Loading an Audio Sample Using the MediaPlayer

The MediaPlayer provides a set of methods to load the media content from various sources such as from an URL (uniform resource locator) or directly from a local file. As shown in Listing 9-12, you can use the setDataSource method to load the media file from a given URL.

Listing 9-12. Loading an Audio Sample into MediaPlayer from a URL

```
MediaPlayer mediaPlayer = new MediaPlayer();
mediaPlayer.setDataSource("http://www.apress.com/sound.mp3");
```

Configuring the Audio Stream of the MediaPlayer

As mentioned earlier in this chapter, to improve the overall user experience, the Android platform categorizes audio streams based on their purpose, such as music and notification. When using the MediaPlayer, the audio stream type for the media content can be specified using the setAudioStreamType[11] method as shown in Listing 9-13.

---

[10]http://developer.android.com/reference/android/media/MediaPlayer.html.
[11]http://developer.android.com/reference/android/media/MediaPlayer.html#setAudioStreamType(int).

Listing 9-13. Setting the Audio Stream Type for MediaPlayer

```
mediaPlayer.setAudioStreamType(AudioManager.STREAM_MUSIC);
```

Preparing the MediaPlayer for Playback

Besides the audio stream type, various aspects of audio playback can be configured through the MediaPlayer. Once all the configuration is done, the application is expected to call the prepare[12] method, as shown in Listing 9-14, in order to get the MediaPlayer prepared for the playback. Once you call the prepare method, you can no longer configure the MediaPlayer.

Listing 9-14. Preparing the MediaPlayer for Playback

```
mediaPlayer.prepare();
```

> **Caution**   While preparing the MediaPlayer for playback, the prepare method also starts the buffering of the media content. As this operation involves an extensive amount of I/O (input/output), it should not be called from the user interface (UI) thread. If MediaPlayer does not have its own dedicated thread, you should use the prepareAsync[13] method instead, in order to prepare the MediaPlayer asynchronously.

Starting the Playback Using the MediaPlayer

Once the MediaPlayer is successfully prepared, the playback can be started anytime using the start[14] method, as shown in Listing 9-15.

Listing 9-15. Starting the Playback Using the MediaPlayer

```
mediaPlayer.start();
```

---

[12]http://developer.android.com/reference/android/media/MediaPlayer.html#prepare().
[13]http://developer.android.com/reference/android/media/MediaPlayer.html#prepareAsync().
[14]http://developer.android.com/reference/android/media/MediaPlayer.html#start().

Stopping the Playback Using the MediaPlayer

Once it is started, the playback can be stopped at any time, using the stop[15] method, as shown in Listing 9-16.

Listing 9-16. Stopping the Playback Using the MediaPlayer

```
mediaPlayer.stop();
```

> **Note**   Once the MediaPlayer is stopped, it needs to be prepared again before it can be restarted.

Releasing the MediaPlayer

Once they are no longer needed, you can release the MediaPlayer resources through the release[16] method, as shown in Listing 9-17.

Listing 9-17. Releasing the MediaPlayer

```
mediaPlayer.release();
```

AsyncPlayer

Loading media content from the network or from the SD card on the UI thread can degrade the performance of the application by makings its UI unresponsive. We recommend using a separate thread to load the content, but it does require more code. For really simple audio playback use cases, the Android framework provides the AsyncPlayer. The AsyncPlayer also relies on the MediaPlayer to do the actual playback. The AsyncPlayer simply runs the MediaPlayer in a separate thread and acts as a bridge between the application and the MediaPlayer. As shown in Listing 9-18, playing an audio sample using the AsyncPlayer is much simpler, and it can be started directly from the UI thread without any problems.

---

[15]http://developer.android.com/reference/android/media/MediaPlayer.html#stop().
[16]http://developer.android.com/reference/android/media/MediaPlayer.html#release().

Listing 9-18. Playing an Audio File Using the AsyncPlayer

```
AsyncPlayer asyncPlayer = new AsyncPlayer("Audio Player");
asyncPlayer.play(this,
        Uri.parse("http://www.apress.com/sound.mp3"),
        false,
        AudioManager.STREAM_MUSIC
);
```

When multiple audio samples need to be played frequently and with low latency, using the AsyncPlayer is not a good solution. The AsyncPlayer can only handle one audio sample at any given time, and running multiple AsyncPlayer instances is not an elegant solution. The Android framework provides the SoundPool just for that purpose.

SoundPool

The Android framework provides SoundPool to manage the audio resources of an application. SoundPool can load a collection of audio samples into memory from the application resources. As the audio samples are already loaded into memory, they can be played anytime with very low latency. Using SoundPool is the best practice for incorporating sound effects into Android applications. SoundPool is exposed through the SoundPool[17] class.

Creating a SoundPool

The procedure to create a new SoundPool has changed starting with the API Level 21 (Android Lollipop 5.0) release.

Creating a SoundPool Using API Level 20 and Below

A new SoundPool can be created by supplying the maximum number of simultaneous audio streams and the stream type to the SoundPool class's constructor, as shown in Listing 9-19.

Listing 9-19. Creating a New SoundPool

```
SoundPool soundPool =
        new SoundPool(2, AudioManager.STREAM_MUSIC, 0);
```

---

[17]http://developer.android.com/reference/android/media/SoundPool.html.

> **Note**   The last argument to the SoundPool class constructor, the
> sample-rate converter quality, currently has no effect. Use 0 for
> the default.

Creating a SoundPool Using API Level 21 and Above

Starting with API Level 21, the Android framework provides a new builder
class, SoundPool.Builder.[18] The builder class facilitates the configuration
of SoundPool by starting with a default configuration and enabling the
application to tune it as necessary. As shown in Listing 9-20, the SoundPool.
Builder also relies on the new AudioAttributes[19] class to allow the
application to specify more information about the audio stream, the purpose
of the audio playback, and how it should be played.

Listing 9-20.   Creating a New SoundPool Using the Builder

```
SoundPool soundPool = new SoundPool.Builder()
    .setMaxStreams(2)
    .setAudioAttributes(
        new AudioAttributes.Builder()
            .setContentType(AudioAttributes.CONTENT_TYPE_MOVIE)
            .setUsage(AudioAttributes.USAGE_MEDIA)
            .build()
    )
    .build();
```

Loading Audio Samples into SoundPool

The SoundPool class provides a set of load methods to load audio samples
from various locations, such as the application resources, the application
assets, and a file. These load methods return a unique identifier, the sound
ID, for each audio sample loaded into SoundPool. This sound ID then can
be used to refer to individual audio samples for playback. The play methods
may return zero as the sound ID to indicate a problem while loading the
audio sample into SoundPool.

---

[18]http://developer.android.com/reference/android/media/SoundPool.Builder.html.
[19]http://developer.android.com/reference/android/media/AudioAttributes.html.

Loading Audio Samples from Application Resources

Audio samples can be loaded from the application resources using the load[20] method, as shown in Listing 9-21. The audio files can be placed in raw resources, and references through the R.raw prefix.

Listing 9-21. Loading an Audio Sample from Application Resources

```
int soundId = soundPool.load(this, R.raw.sound, 1);
```

Loading Audio Samples from Application Assets

Audio samples can be loaded from the application assets using the load[21] method, as shown in Listing 9-22. The audio files can be placed in the assets directory and accessed through the AssetManager class.

Listing 9-22. Loading an Audio Sample from Application Assets

```
int soundId = soundPool.load(
        getAssets().openFd("sound.mp3"),
        1);
```

Loading Audio Samples from Files

Audio samples can also be loaded directly from files by providing the file path to the load[22] method, as shown in Listing 9-23.

Listing 9-23. Loading an Audio Sample from a File

```
int soundId = soundPool.load("/sdcard/sound.mp3", 1);
```

Playing Audio Samples from SoundPool

Once the audio samples are loaded into the sound play, they can be played anytime using the play[23] method by simply providing the sound ID for the audio sample to play, as shown in Listing 9-24. The play method also takes additional parameters, such as the volume, the stream priority, the loop mode, and the playback rate.

---

[20]http://developer.android.com/reference/android/media/SoundPool. html#load(android.content.Context, int, int).
[21]http://developer.android.com/reference/android/media/SoundPool. html#load(android.content.res.AssetFileDescriptor, int).
[22]http://developer.android.com/reference/android/media/SoundPool. html#load(java.lang.String, int).
[23]http://developer.android.com/reference/android/media/SoundPool. html#play(int, float, float, int, int, float).

Listing 9-24. Playing an Audio Sample Using SoundPool

```
soundPool.play(
        soundId, // sound id
        1,       // left volume set to max
        1,       // right volume set to max
        0,       // low priority audio stream
        0,       // don't loop
        1        // default rate
);
```

If the play method is successful, it returns a non-zero stream ID. This stream ID can be used to tune some of the playback parameters while the audio is playing. For example, if the loop mode is requested, the application can terminate the playback by invoking the stop[24] method and providing the stream ID to stop.

Unloading an Audio Sample from SoundPool

As indicated in the section "Loading Audio Samples into SoundPool," SoundPool loads the audio samples into memory in order to be able to play them with a low latency. As memory is a scarce resource on the Android platform, applications should take the necessary caution to manage memory appropriately. If an audio sample will no longer be used, the application can use the unload method, as shown in Listing 9-25, to remove it from SoundPool in order to free memory.

Listing 9-25. Unloading an Audio Sample from SoundPool

```
soundPool.unload(soundId);
```

Releasing SoundPool

If SoundPool is no longer needed, the application code should explicitly release it using the release method, as shown in Listing 9-26. Application developers should not entirely rely on garbage collection to do the job.

Listing 9-26. Releasing SoundPool

```
soundPool.release();
```

---

[24]http://developer.android.com/reference/android/media/SoundPool.html#stop(int).

Recording Audio

Besides the audio playback, the Android framework also provides the functionality to record audio, using the MediaRecorder[25] class.

Requesting Audio Record Permission

For the application to record audio, it is required to have the android.permission.RECORD_AUDIO[26] permission. The application can request this permission through its AndroidManifest.xml file as shown in Listing 9-27.

Listing 9-27. Requesting Audio Record Permission

```
<uses-permission android:name="android.permission.RECORD_AUDIO" />
```

Configuring the Audio Source for Recording

The audio source for recording can be set through the setAudioSource[27] method, as shown in Listing 9-28.

Listing 9-28. Using the Microphone as the Audio Source

```
MediaRecorder mediaRecorder = new MediaRecorder();
mediaRecorder.setAudioSource(MediaRecorder.AudioSource.MIC);
```

The MediaRecorder.AudioSource[28] class contains the constants for each supported audio source.

- CAMCORDER: Microphone audio source with same orientation as camera if supported by the device.
- DEFAULT: Default audio source.
- MIC: Microphone audio source.
- REMOTE_SUBMIX: Audio source for submix of audio streams.

[25]http://developer.android.com/reference/android/media/MediaRecorder.html.
[26]http://developer.android.com/reference/android/Manifest.permission.html#RECORD_AUDIO.
[27]http://developer.android.com/reference/android/media/MediaRecorder.html#setAudioSource(int).
[28]http://developer.android.com/reference/android/media/MediaRecorder.AudioSource.html.

- VOICE_CALL: Voice call uplink and downlink audio.

- VOICE_COMMUNICATION: Microphone that is tuned for voice communications.

- VOICE_DOWNLINK: Voice call downlink audio.

- VOICE_RECOGNITION: Microphone that is tuned for voice recognition.

- VOICE_UPLINK: Voice call uplink audio.

Configuring the Audio Output for Recording

The recorded audio should be stored in a file using an audio encoder and a compatible container format. The list of supported audio encoders and the corresponding container formats can be found in the section "Core Media Formats[29]" in the Android developer pages.

Configuring the Audio Encoder for Recording

The recorded audio must be compressed using an audio encoder. The setAudioEncoder[30] method allows the application to choose an audio encoder to use for recording, as shown in Listing 9-29.

Listing 9-29. Setting the Audio Encoder for Recording

```
mediaRecorder.setAudioEncoder(
    MediaRecorder.AudioEncoder.AMR_NB);
```

The MediaRecorder.AudioEncoder[31] class contains the constants for each of the supported audio encoders.

Configuring the Output File Container Format

The encoded audio must be placed into a file. The setOutputFormat[32] method can be used to specify the container format, as shown in Listing 9-30.

---

[29]http://developer.android.com/guide/appendix/media-formats.html.
[30]http://developer.android.com/reference/android/media/MediaRecorder.html#setAudioEncoder(int).
[31]http://developer.android.com/reference/android/media/MediaRecorder.AudioEncoder.html.
[32]http://developer.android.com/reference/android/media/MediaRecorder.html#setOutputFormat(int).

Listing 9-30. Configuring the Output File Container Format

```
mediaRecorder.setOutputFormat(
    MediaRecorder.OutputFormat.THREE_GPP);
```

The MediaRecorder.OutputFormat[33] class provides constants for each of the supported container types.

Configuring the Output File

The output file can be set through the setOutputFile[34] method, as shown in Listing 9-31. The file extension should match the container format that is specified.

Listing 9-31. Configuring the Output File

```
mediaRecorder.setOutputFile("/sdcard/sound.3gp");
```

Starting the Audio Recording

Once the MediaRecorder is configured, it can be prepared for recording using the prepare[35] method. The audio recording can then be started using the start[36] method as shown in Listing 9-32.

Listing 9-32. Starting the Audio Recording

```
mediaRecorder.prepare();
mediaRecorder.start();
```

Stopping the Audio Recording

The audio recording can be stopped anytime using the stop[37] method as shown in Listing 9-33.

---

[33]http://developer.android.com/reference/android/media/MediaRecorder.
OutputFormat.html.
[34]http://developer.android.com/reference/android/media/MediaRecorder.
html#setOutputFile(java.lang.String).
[35]http://developer.android.com/reference/android/media/MediaRecorder.
html#prepare().
[36]http://developer.android.com/reference/android/media/MediaRecorder.
html#start().
[37]http://developer.android.com/reference/android/media/MediaRecorder.
html#stop().

Listing 9-33. Stopping the Audio Recording

```
mediaRecorder.stop();
```

Releasing the MediaRecorder

Once the MediaRecorder is no longer needed, it can be released using the release[38] method as shown in Listing 9-34

Listing 9-34. Releasing the MediaRecorder

```
mediaRecorder.release();
```

Playing Video

The MediaPlayer class, covered in the section "Playing Audio," also provides video playbook support. As the API provided through the MediaPlayer class is very generic, the same API call sequence applies to both audio and video playback. Besides these API calls, the video playback also requires a valid Surface[39] to draw the video frames.

Creating a Surface for Video Playback

Surface support is provided through the UI component SurfaceView.[40] SurfaceView can be incorporated into an existing UI layout as shown in Listing 9-35.

Listing 9-35. Adding a SurfaceView to UI Layout

```
<SurfaceView
    android:id="@+id/surface"
    android:layout_width="match_parent"
    android:layout_height="match_parent" />
```

---

[38]http://developer.android.com/reference/android/media/MediaRecorder.html#release().
[39]http://developer.android.com/reference/android/view/Surface.html.
[40]http://developer.android.com/reference/android/view/SurfaceView.html.

SurfaceView is simply a view holder around the actual Surface object. Compared to the other UI widgets provided by the Android framework, the initialization of the Surface object is not guaranteed to happen when the onCreate or onResume method of the activity gets invoked as part of the Activity life cycle. The application is expected to register, in the Activity's onCreate method, to receive the Surface life-cycle events through the SurfaceView's SurfaceHolder,[41] as shown in Listing 9-36.

Listing 9-36. Registering to Receive for Surface Life-Cycle Events

```
SurfaceView surfaceView =
    (SurfaceView) findViewById(R.id.surface);

surfaceView.getHolder().addCallback(
        new SurfaceHolder.Callback() {
    @Override
    public void surfaceCreated(SurfaceHolder surfaceHolder) {
        startPlayback(surfaceHolder);
    }

    @Override
    public void surfaceChanged(SurfaceHolder surfaceHolder,
            int i, int i2, int i3) {

    }

    @Override
    public void surfaceDestroyed(SurfaceHolder surfaceHolder) {
        stopPlayback();
    }
});
```

Starting Video Playback

When Surface becomes available, the application will get informed through the surfaceCreated[42] callback method. Within this callback, the application can extract the valid Surface object from the provided SurfaceHolder object through its getSurface[43] method, as shown in Listing 9-37.

---

[41]http://developer.android.com/reference/android/view/SurfaceHolder.html.
[42]http://developer.android.com/reference/android/view/SurfaceHolder.
Callback.html#surfaceCreated(android.view.SurfaceHolder).
[43]http://developer.android.com/reference/android/view/SurfaceHolder.
html#getSurface().

Listing 9-37. Starting the Video Playback When the Surface Is Available

```
private void startPlayback(SurfaceHolder surfaceHolder) {
    mediaPlayer = new MediaPlayer();
    mediaPlayer.setSurface(surfaceHolder.getSurface());
    mediaPlayer.setScreenOnWhilePlaying(true);

    try {
        mediaPlayer.setDataSource(
                "http://www.apress.com/movie.mp4");
    } catch (IOException e) {
        e.printStackTrace();
        releasePlayer();
        return;
    }

    mediaPlayer.setOnPreparedListener(
            new MediaPlayer.OnPreparedListener() {
            @Override
            public void onPrepared(MediaPlayer mediaPlayer) {
                mediaPlayer.start();
            }
    });

    mediaPlayer.prepareAsync();
}
```

Stopping Video Playback

As shown in Listing 9-38, the video playback can be stopped at any time using the MediaPlayer APIs discussed in the section "Playing Audio."

Listing 9-38. Stopping the Video Playback and Releasing the MediaPlayer

```
private void stopPlayback() {
    if (mediaPlayer != null) {
        mediaPlayer.stop();
        releasePlayer();
    }
}

private void releasePlayer() {
    mediaPlayer.release();
    mediaPlayer = null;
}
```

Video Recording

The same as the audio recording, the video recording is also handled by the MediaRecorder. The MediaRecorder requires a valid Surface to display the preview during the video recording.

Creating a Preview Surface for Video Recording

Refer to the section "Creating a Surface for Video Playback" for the steps that are necessary to create and use the Surface object. The preview surface can be configured using the setPreviewDisplay[44] method, as shown in Listing 9-39.

Listing 9-39. Setting the Preview Surface for Video Recording

```
mediaRecorder.setPreviewDisplay(surfaceHolder.getSurface());
```

Configuring the Video Source for Video Recording

The MediaRecorder can record directly from the device's camera, or from another Surface object. The MediaRecorder.VideoSource[45] class provides constants for each of the available video sources. The video source can be set using the setVideoSource[46] method, as shown in Listing 9-40.

Listing 9-40. Setting the Video Source for Video Recording

```
mediaRecorder.setVideoSource(MediaRecorder.VideoSource.CAMERA);
```

---

[44]http://developer.android.com/reference/android/media/MediaRecorder.
html#setPreviewDisplay(android.view.Surface).
[45]http://developer.android.com/reference/android/media/MediaRecorder.
VideoSource.html.
[46]http://developer.android.com/reference/android/media/MediaRecorder.
html#setVideoSource(int).

Configuring the Video Encoder for Video Recording

The recorded video should be encoded using a video encoder for proper compression. The MediaRecorder.VideoEncoder[47] class provides constants for each of the support video encoders on the Android platform. The setVideoEncoder[48] method can be used to set the video encoder as shown in Listing 9-41.

Listing 9-41. Setting the Video Encoder for Video Recording

```
mediaRecorder.setVideoEncoder(
        MediaRecorder.VideoEncoder.MPEG_4_SP);
```

Camera

Android devices are mostly equipped with one or more cameras. Typical Android phones have both a front and back camera, allowing the applications to capture pictures and videos. The Android framework provides a comprehensive set of APIs to interact with these cameras.

Requesting the Camera Access Permission

For the application to be able to interact with the camera, it is required to have the android.permission.CAMERA[49] permission. As shown in Listing 9-42, this permission can be requested through the uses-permission XML tag in the AndroidManifest.xml file.

Listing 9-42. Requesting the Camera Access Permission

```
<uses-permission android:name="android.permission.CAMERA" />
```

In addition to the android.permission.CAMERA permission, the application should also declare use of the android.hardware.camera2 feature through the uses-feature XML tag in the AndroidManifest.xml file as shown in Listing 9-43.

---

[47]http://developer.android.com/reference/android/media/MediaRecorder.
VideoEncoder.html.
[48]http://developer.android.com/reference/android/media/MediaRecorder.
html#setVideoEncoder(int).
[49]http://developer.android.com/reference/android/Manifest.permission.
html#CAMERA.

Listing 9-43. Declaring the Use of the Camera Feature

```
<uses-feature android:name="android.hardware.camera2"
              android:required="false" />
```

If the application can use the camera, but the camera is not required for the application to function, the android:required attribute of the uses-feature XML tag can be set to false. Otherwise, Google Play will prevent the application from being installed on devices without a camera.

CameraManager

Starting with Android 5.0 Lollipop, the CameraManager[50] class and supporting classes in the android.hardware.camera2 package provide the camera API on the Android platform. You can obtain an instance of the CameraManager class through the getSystemService method of the current Context, as shown in Listing 9-44.

Listing 9-44. Getting an Instance of the CameraManager

```
CameraManager cameraManager =
        (CameraManager) getSystemService(Context.CAMERA_SERVICE);
```

Getting the Cameras IDs

Since the device can have multiple cameras, the application can use the getCameraIdList method of the CameraManager class to get a list of IDs for the available cameras, as shown in Listing 9-45.

Listing 9-45. Getting the IDs of the Available Cameras

```
try {
    String[] cameraIds = cameraManager.getCameraIdList();
} catch (CameraAccessException e) {
    // Access exception
}
```

50

Getting the Camera Characteristics

Based on the camera ID, the application can get the camera characteristics through the getCameraCharacteristics[51] method of the CameraManager class, as shown in Listing 9-46.

Listing 9-46. Getting the Camera Characteristics

```
String[] cameraIds = cameraManager.getCameraIdList();
for (String cameraId : cameraIds) {
    CameraCharacteristics cameraCharacteristics =
            cameraManager.getCameraCharacteristics(cameraId);

    if (CameraCharacteristics.LENS_FACING_FRONT ==
            cameraCharacteristics.get(CameraCharacteristics.LENS_FACING)) {
        // Found front facing camera
    }
}
```

It returns a CameraCharacteristics[52] instance that contains the camera information as key and value pairs. The CameraCharacteristics class provides a set of key constants for the standard camera characteristics that can be queried through its get[53] method. The most notable ones are

- LENS_FACING: Direction of the camera relative to the device. It can be either LENS_FACING_FRONT for the front-facing camera or LENS_FACING_BACK for the back camera.

- SCALER_STREAM_CONFIGURATION_MAP: Available stream configurations that are supported. Returns a StreamConfigurationMap[54] instance. It contains supported formats and sizes.

---

[51]http://developer.android.com/reference/android/hardware/camera2/
CameraManager.html#getCameraCharacteristics(java.lang.String).
[52]http://developer.android.com/reference/android/hardware/camera2/
CameraCharacteristics.html.
[53]http://developer.android.com/reference/android/hardware/
camera2/CameraCharacteristics.html#get(android.hardware.camera2.
CameraCharacteristics.Key<T>).
[54]http://developer.android.com/reference/android/hardware/camera2/
params/StreamConfigurationMap.html.

Opening the Camera

The application can open the camera through the openCamera[55] method of the CameraManager class. Upon calling this method, the StateCallback[56] interface delivers the result to the application. The following callback methods must be implemented by the application:

- onOpened: Called when the camera has finished opening.

- onError: Called when the camera device encountered an error:

  - ERROR_CAMERA_DEVICE: Camera device encountered a fatal error.

  - ERROR_CAMERA_DISABLED: Camera could not be opened due to device policy.

  - ERROR_CAMERA_IN_USE: Camera is in use already by another application.

  - ERROR_CAMERA_SERVICE: Camera service encountered a fatal error.

  - ERROR_MAX_CAMERAS_IN_USE: There are too many open camera devices.

- onDisconnect: Called when the camera device is no longer available.

- onClosed: Called when the camera device is closed.

The openCamera method takes the ID of the camera, a StateCallback instance, and the handler instance to use for invoking the callback interface, as shown in Listing 9-47.

---

[55]http://developer.android.com/reference/android/hardware/camera2/CameraManager.html#openCamera(java.lang.String,%20android.hardware.camera2.CameraDevice.StateCallback,%20android.os.Handler).
[56]http://developer.android.com/reference/android/hardware/camera2/CameraDevice.StateCallback.html.

> **Note**　Although the handler is set to null on code examples in this
> section for simplicity, we strongly recommend that you use a dedicated
> Handler[57] instance for processing the asynchronous camera requests.
> You can create a dedicated Handler by using the HandlerThread[58]
> class.

Listing 9-47.　Opening the Camera Device

```
cameraManager.openCamera(cameraId, new CameraDevice.StateCallback() {
    @Override
    public void onOpened(CameraDevice camera) {
        // Camera opened
    }

    @Override
    public void onDisconnected(CameraDevice camera) {
        // Camera disconnected
    }

    @Override
    public void onError(CameraDevice camera, int error) {
        // Camera error
    }
},
null);
```

Capturing from the Camera

In order to be able to capture from the camera, a Surface instance is
needed. I explain the steps to obtain a Surface instance in the section
"Playing Video." Both the Surface instance and the camera should be
configured prior to starting the camera capture.

---

[57]http://developer.android.com/reference/android/os/Handler.html.
[58]http://developer.android.com/reference/android/os/HandlerThread.html.

Getting the Supported Camera Output Sizes

You must obtain the required output size of the camera through the
CameraCharacteristics using the SCALER_STREAM_CONFIGURATION_MAP key.
The retrieved value is an instance of StreamConfigurationMap[59] class. The
getOutputSizes method returns a list of supported camera output sizes
(see Listing 9-48).

Listing 9-48. Getting the Supported Output Sizes

```
StreamConfigurationMap streamConfigurationMap = cameraCharacteristics.get(
        CameraCharacteristics.SCALER_STREAM_CONFIGURATION_MAP);

Size[] outputSizes = streamConfigurationMap.getOutputSizes(SurfaceHolder.
class);
```

Setting the Size of the Camera Preview Surface

The size of the Surface must be set to one of the supported output sizes
through the setFixedSize method of the SurfaceHolder class, as shown in
Listing 9-49.

Listing 9-49. Setting the Size of the Surface to a Supported Output Size

```
surfaceHolder.setFixedSize(
        outputSizes[0].getWidth(),
        outputSizes[0].getHeight());
```

Creating a Camera Capture Session

Once the Surface is created and resized properly, the application can
create a camera session through the createCaptureSession[60] method of the
CameraDevice instance, as shown in Listing 9-50.

---

[59]http://developer.android.com/reference/android/hardware/camera2/
params/StreamConfigurationMap.html#getOutputSizes(java.lang.Class<T>).
[60]https://developer.android.com/reference/android/hardware/camera2/
CameraDevice.html#createCaptureSession(java.util.List<android.view.
Surface>, android.hardware.camera2.CameraCaptureSession.StateCallback,
android.os.Handler).

Listing 9-50. Creating a Camera Capture Session

```
Surface surface = surfaceHolder.getSurface();

cameraDevice.createCaptureSession(Arrays.asList(surface),
        new CameraCaptureSession.StateCallback() {
    @Override
    public void onConfigured(CameraCaptureSession session) {

    }

    @Override
    public void onConfigureFailed(CameraCaptureSession session) {

    }
}, null);
```

The createCaptureSession method takes a list of Surface instances that will be used during this camera session, a subclass of the CameraCaptureSession.StateCallback[61], and a handler to use. The result of the method call gets delivered to the application through the methods of the provided CameraCaptureSession.StateCallback subclass. In order to subclass it, the application should provide implementations of the following callback methods:

- onConfigured: Camera capture session is successfully created, and it can start processing capture requests.

- onConfigurationFailed: Camera capture session could not be started.

Create a Capture Request

Once you create the camera capture session, it can process multiple camera capture requests. The createCaptureRequest[62] method of the CameraDevice instance creates the camera capture requests. The createCaptureRequest is a helper method. For the most frequently used camera capture requests, the Android framework provides templates to minimize the coding needed.

---

[61]https://developer.android.com/reference/android/hardware/camera2/CameraCaptureSession.StateCallback.html.
[62]https://developer.android.com/reference/android/hardware/camera2/CameraDevice.html#createCaptureRequest(int).

- TEMPLATE_MANUAL: Basic template for direct application control of capture request.

- TEMPLATE_PREVIEW: Request suitable for camera preview.

- TEMPLATE_RECORD: Request suitable for video recording.

- TEMPLATE_STILL_CAPTURE: Request suitable for still image capture.

- TEMPLATE_VIDEO_SNAPSHOT: Request suitable for still image capture while recording.

- TEMPLATE_ZERO_SHUTTER_LAG: Request suitable for zero shutter lag still image capture.

The createCaptureRequest method takes a template type and returns a CaptureRequest.Builder instance, as shown in Listing 9-51.

Listing 9-51. Creating a Camera Capture Request Builder

```
CaptureRequest.Builder previewRequestBuilder =
      cameraDevice.createCaptureRequest(CameraDevice.TEMPLATE_PREVIEW);
```

Adding the Target Surface

Every camera capture request requires a target Surface. This target Surface also must be one of the Surface instances that are provided earlier when creating the camera capture session. The target Surface for a camera capture request can be set through the addTarget[63] method of the CaptureRequest.Builder instance, as shown in Listing 9-52.

Listing 9-52. Adding the Target Surface to the Camera Preview Request Builder

```
previewRequestBuilder.addTarget(surfaceHolder.getSurface());
```

Additional CameraCaptureRequest Configuration

The application can do further configuration for the capture request using this builder instance, as shown in Listing 9-53.

Listing 9-53. Setting the Auto-Focus Mode to Continuous Video for the Camera Capture Request

```
previewRequestBuilder.set(CaptureRequest.CONTROL_AF_MODE,
      CaptureRequest.CONTROL_AF_MODE_CONTINUOUS_VIDEO);
```

---

[63]https://developer.android.com/reference/android/hardware/camera2/
CaptureRequest.Builder.html#addTarget(android.view.Surface).

The list of supported capture request keys varies. The list of supported ones by the device can be obtained through the getAvailableCaptureRequestKeys[64] method of the CameraCharacteristics class. Constant values are provided in the CaptureRequest[65] class for the most standard ones. Some of those are

- COLOR_CORRECTION_MODE: How the image data is converted from the camera sensor's native colorspace into linear sRGB colorspace.

- CONTROL_AE_MODE: Desired mode for auto-exposure.

- CONTROL_AF_MODE: Desired mode for auto-focus.

- CONTROL_AWB_MODE: Desired mode for auto-white-balance.

- CONTROL_EFFECT_MODE: Special color effects to apply.

- FLASH_MODE: Desired mode for camera flash.

- JPEG_QUALITY: Compression quality for the JPEG image for still image capture.

- SCALER_CROP_REGION: Desired portion of the image to read out of this capture.

- SENSOR_SENSITIVITY: Amount of gain to apply to sensor data before processing.

Building the CameraCaptureRequest

Once the capture request is fully configured, the application can invoke the build method of the CaptureRequest.Builder instance to create the actual camera capture request, as shown in Listing 9-54.

Listing 9-54. Building the Camera Capture Request

```
CaptureRequest previewRequest = previewRequestBuilder.build();
```

---

[64]https://developer.android.com/reference/android/hardware/camera2/
CameraCharacteristics.html#getAvailableCaptureRequestKeys().
[65]https://developer.android.com/reference/android/hardware/camera2/
CaptureRequest.html.

Submitting the CameraCaptureRequest

The CameraCaptureSession class provides a set of methods to allow submitting the CameraCaptureRequest instances for processing.

- ▓ capture[66]: Submit the request for a single image to be captured from the camera.

- ▓ captureBurst[67]: Submit the given list of requests to be captured in sequence as a burst.

- ▓ setRepeatingRequest[68]: Submit the request for endless repeating capture of images (e.g., for the camera preview).

- ▓ setRepeatingBurst[69]: Submit the given list of requests to be endlessly captured in sequence as a burst.

These methods also take a CameraCaptureSession.CaptureCallback[70] instance to inform the application regarding the status of the request, as shown in Listing 9-55.

Listing 9-55. Submit the Camera Preview Request as a Repeating Request

```
session.setRepeatingRequest(previewRequest,
        new CameraCaptureSession.CaptureCallback() {
    @Override
    public void onCaptureCompleted(
```

[66]https://developer.android.com/reference/android/hardware/camera2/
CameraCaptureSession.html#capture(android.hardware.camera2.
CaptureRequest, android.hardware.camera2.CameraCaptureSession.
CaptureCallback, android.os.Handler).
[67]https://developer.android.com/reference/android/hardware/camera2/
CameraCaptureSession.html#captureBurst(java.util.List<android.hardware.
camera2.CaptureRequest>, android.hardware.camera2.CameraCaptureSession.
CaptureCallback, android.os.Handler).
[68]https://developer.android.com/reference/android/hardware/camera2/
CameraCaptureSession.html#setRepeatingRequest(android.hardware.
camera2.CaptureRequest, android.hardware.camera2.CameraCaptureSession.
CaptureCallback, android.os.Handler).
[69]https://developer.android.com/reference/android/hardware/camera2/
CameraCaptureSession.html#setRepeatingBurst(java.util.List<android.
hardware.camera2.CaptureRequest>, android.hardware.camera2.
CameraCaptureSession.CaptureCallback, android.os.Handler).
[70]https://developer.android.com/reference/android/hardware/camera2/
CameraCaptureSession.CaptureCallback.html.

```
        CameraCaptureSession session,
        CaptureRequest request,
        TotalCaptureResult result) {
    super.onCaptureCompleted(session, request, result);
    // Capture completed
    }
}, null);
```

The repeating capture requests can be terminated at any given time through the stopRepeating[71] method of the CameraCaptureSession instance.

Summary

This section briefly explored the multimedia support provided by the Android platform. Android differentiates between audio streams based on their purpose and allows each of these stream groups to be controlled individually for a superior user experience. AudioManager provides APIs to tune different aspects of each of these audio streams, as well as the audio input and output components of the device. Audio playback has various use cases and also unique challenges. The Android platform provides various APIs to address the most frequent use cases. The MediaPlayer API allows the application to play media streams with fine control. Meanwhile, the SoundPool API allows the application to pre-load the small and frequently used audio samples into memory for low-latency playback. The Android framework also provides the MediaRecorder API for recording both audio and video stream from various sources. At last, the chapter also provides a brief overview of the new Camera API that is provided with the Android 5.0 Lollipop version (API Level 21).

---

[71]https://developer.android.com/reference/android/hardware/camera2/
CameraCaptureSession.html#stopRepeating().

Index

Get the eBook for only $10!

Now you can take the weightless companion with you anywhere, anytime. Your purchase of this book entitles you to 3 electronic versions for only $10.

This Apress title will prove so indispensible that you'll want to carry it with you everywhere, which is why we are offering the eBook in 3 formats for only $10 if you have already purchased the print book.

Convenient and fully searchable, the PDF version enables you to easily find and copy code—or perform examples by quickly toggling between instructions and applications. The MOBI format is ideal for your Kindle, while the ePUB can be utilized on a variety of mobile devices.

Go to www.apress.com/promo/tendollars to purchase your companion eBook.

Printed in the United States
By Bookmasters